Claire

Secondary Mathematics 1
Problems and Practice

Ian Moir

Principal Teacher of Mathematics
Keith Grammar School

Oxford University Press 1986

Oxford University Press, Walton Street, Oxford OX2 6DP

Oxford New York Toronto
Delhi Bombay Calcutta Madras Karachi
Petaling Jaya Singapore Hong Kong Tokyo
Nairobi Dar es Salaam Cape Town
Melbourne Auckland

and associated companies in
Beirut Berlin Ibadan Nicosia

Oxford is a trade mark of Oxford University Press

ISBN 0 19 833690 X

© Oxford University Press 1986
First published 1986

Typeset by Quadra Graphics, Oxford
Printed in Great Britain by
Butler & Tanner Ltd, Frome and London

Preface

This series of four books is intended for the majority of pupils in the first years of secondary schooling. It provides a firm basis in the mathematics needed for Standard Grade in Scotland and for GCSE examinations. The books can be used either as a complete course or as a supplement to existing textbooks.

Each section of this book includes brief teaching notes and worked examples followed by ample practice which is carefully graded. Whilst some of the material derives from the successful *Comprehensive Mathematics Practice*, much has been added to satisfy the requirements of pupils aiming at Standard Grade and at GCSE. Wherever possible, stress is laid on practical or topical aspects of the subject, with a large number of questions relating, through ordinary language, to the everyday experience and interests of the pupils. The series also includes many investigations which emphasise both the development of problem solving abilities and the links between mathematics and the real world.

The questions cover a wide range of abilities, and will be particularly suitable for use with mixed ability classes. The series is designed to provide a relevant and lively course which should encourage all pupils to gain confidence in their mathematical abilities and to reach their highest possible level of performance.

The numerical answers to the questions in all four books are provided in a separate answer book.

Thanks are due to the authors of *Comprehensive Mathematics Practice* for their inspiration and help in the preparation of this new series.

Ian Moir

Contents

1 Number

1.1 Number

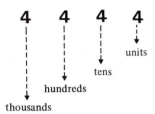

The number shown above is made up of 4 thousands, 4 hundreds, 4 tens and 4 units.
It is the number four thousand four hundred and forty-four.
You will see that the value of each 4 depends upon its position, that is its place value.

Example 1

Write down the following numbers in words.

a) 234   b) 6070
c) 4762   d) 8088

a) two hundred and thirty-four.
b) six thousand and seventy.
c) four thousand seven hundred and sixty-two.
d) eight thousand and eighty-eight.

Exercise 1

Write the following numbers in words.

1. 4	2. 11	3. 13	4. 17
5. 29	6. 32	7. 56	8. 70
9. 85	10. 98		

11. 104	12. 140	13. 270	14. 295
15. 354	16. 526	17. 681	18. 712
19. 837	20. 916		

21. 1001	22. 1010	23. 1984	24. 2300
25. 2320	26. 3071	27. 4040	28. 5500
29. 7859	30. 9099		

31. 4653	32. 8097	33. 6712	34. 7304
35. 5410	36. 8934	37. 9090	38. 2400
39. 1204	40. 4008		

41. Write in words:
a) the altitude of Beattock Summit,
b) its distance from Glasgow,
c) its distance from London.

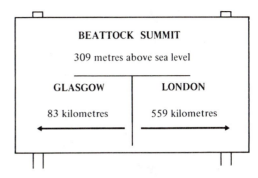

42. Write in words the length of the Mersey Tunnel.

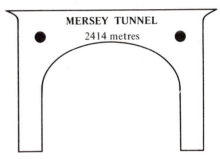

43. Write in words:
a) the distance from Liverpool to New York,
b) the distance from Southampton to Panama,
c) the distance from London to Cape Town.

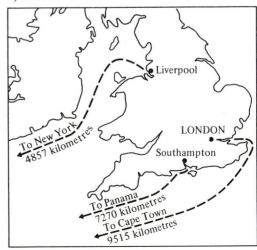

Exercise 2

Write the following numbers in figures

1. eight
2. thirteen
3. seventeen
4. nineteen
5. twenty
6. thirty-one
7. forty-two
8. fifty-five
9. seventy-two
10. eighty-five

11. one hundred and ninety
12. four hundred and sixty
13. four hundred and sixty-seven
14. eight hundred and ten
15. eight hundred and twelve
16. seven hundred and four
17. nine hundred and one
18. six thousand five hundred
19. six thousand five hundred and twenty
20. nine thousand one hundred and thirty

21. three thousand six hundred and nineteen
22. three thousand six hundred and two
23. eight thousand seven hundred and six
24. eight thousand and ninety-one
25. one thousand and fifty-six
26. one thousand and fifty
27. four thousand and ten
28. four thousand and four
29. eight thousand and eleven
30. seventeen hundred and fifty

31. eighteen hundred and five
32. nineteen hundred and eighty-four
33. seven thousand and seventy-two

In questions **34** to **40**, a number is written in a sentence. Rewrite the number in figures.

34. There are seven hundred and thirty-six pupils at Manor Hill School.
35. Queen Elizabeth II was crowned eight hundred and eighty-seven years after the Norman Conquest.
36. Nine thousand one hundred and twenty-one spectators were at the football match last Saturday.
37. The population of Leominster is seven thousand two hundred and six.
38. The summit of Snowdon is one thousand and eighty-five metres above sea level.
39. Queen Elizabeth II was crowned in nineteen hundred and fifty-three.
40. The last battle in Britain was fought in seventeen hundred and forty-six.

Example 2

Give the value of each underlined figure.

a) 4**8**3   b) 2**0**04

a) eight tens or eighty
b) 0 hundreds or 0

Exercise 3

Give the value of each underlined figure.

1. 1**1**
2. 1**6**
3. 32**5**
4. 3**5**3
5. 6**0**7
6. 4**3**1
7. 6**5**0
8. **3**31
9. **9**80
10. **5**01

11. 437**6**
12. 925**2**
13. 5**4**07
14. 900**2**
15. 21**7**5
16. 35**1**4
17. 71**6**0
18. 80**5**0
19. 19**3**7
20. 3**1**06

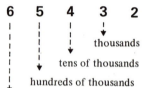

|6|5|4|3|2|1|0|

thousands
tens of thousands
hundreds of thousands
millions

The number above is made up of 6 millions, 5 hundreds of thousands, 4 tens of thousands, 3 thousands, 2 hundreds and 1 ten.

It is the number
six million, five hundred and forty-three thousand, two hundred and ten.

Exercise 4

Give the value of each underlined figure.

1. 4**3**00
2. 5**2**37
3. **8**025
4. **1**010
5. **9**999
6. 8946
7. 785**2**
8. 10 40**2**
9. 1**5** 050
10. 4**3** 620

11. **6**804
12. 94**1**0
13. 7**6**29
14. 22**6**40
15. **3**7 609
16. **2**10 405
17. 35**2** 614
18. **7**64 200
19. 2**5**06 709
20. **8**641 902
21. 4**3**08 207

Example 3

Arrange the following numbers in order of size, starting with the *smallest*.

three hundred and ten, thirty-seven, three hundred and four, forty-three, one hundred and eighty-nine

The numbers in figures are 310, 37, 304, 43, 189

The order is: 37, 43, 189, 304, 310

Exercise 5

Arrange the following numbers in order of size, starting with the *smallest*. Give your answers in figures.

1. 5, 9, 11, 6, 4.
2. 16, 12, 19, 17, 14.
3. 44, 42, 51, 49, 43.
4. 70, 72, 71, 73, 75.
5. 45, 40, 55, 54, 50.
6. 132, 113, 123, 121, 112.
7. 112, 110, 109, 120, 99.
8. 432, 423, 412, 433, 421.
9. 140, 104, 144, 49, 114.
10. 1001, 890, 1010, 980, 110.

11. five hundred and thirty, five hundred and forty, five hundred and five, five hundred and four, five hundred and thirty-four.
12. seven hundred and eighty-six, six hundred and eighty-seven, six hundred and seventy-eight, seven hundred and sixty-eight, eight hundred and seventy-six.
13. two thousand two hundred and thirty-one, two thousand three hundred and twenty-one, two thousand one hundred and twenty-three, two thousand one hundred and thirty-two, two thousand three hundred and twelve.
14. one thousand and sixty-one, one thousand and sixteen, one thousand one hundred and six, one thousand and six, one thousand and sixty.
15. four thousand and forty, four thousand four hundred and four, four thousand and four, four thousand four hundred, four thousand and forty-four.
16. eighty-eight, 99, 98, 89, ninety.
17. 180, one hundred and eight, 88, eighty, one hundred and eighteen.
18. 113, one hundred and thirty, 133, one hundred and three, 123.

19. 250, two hundred and twenty, two hundred and fifteen, 225, two hundred and fifty-five.
20. 606, six hundred and sixty, 665, six hundred and five, 650.

Example 4

Arrange the following numbers in order of size, starting with the *largest*.

273, forty-six, 9126, three thousand and two, 7.

The order is: 9126, 3002, 273, 46, 7

Exercise 6

Arrange the following numbers in order of size, starting with the *largest*. Give your answers in figures.

1. 64, 69, 61, 63, 66.
2. 108, 89, 111, 198, 189.
3. 254, 268, 245, 256, 286.
4. 1012, 1210, 1021, 2101, 1102.
5. 6462, 4662, 6642, 6426, 4626.
6. seventy-eight, seventy-five, eighty-seven, fifty-seven, forty-eight.
7. two hundred and four, two hundred and forty, two hundred and forty-two, two hundred and twenty-two, two hundred and forty-four.
8. four thousand and sixty, four thousand six hundred, four thousand six hundred and forty, four thousand and sixty-four, four thousand six hundred and six.
9. eight hundred and eighty, eight hundred and forty-eight, eight hundred and eighty-four, eight hundred and thirty-four, eight hundred and eighty-eight.
10. one thousand and one, one thousand and eleven, one thousand one hundred and ten, one thousand one hundred and one, one thousand and ten.

11. forty-five, 55, fifty-six, 54, 44.
12. ninety-nine, 109, one hundred and nineteen, 94, one hundred and four.
13. 105, one hundred and fifty, 120, one hundred and twenty-five, 155.
14. 330, three hundred and thirty-two, three hundred and fifty, 352, three hundred and forty-two.
15. 440, four hundred and four, 444, 414, four hundred and forty-one.
16. 10 462, eleven thousand, 1406, eight hundred, 10 100.
17. one thousand four hundred, 1350, sixteen hundred and ten, 1456, 1650.

18. ten thousand six hundred and one, 10 062, twenty thousand and twenty, nineteen hundred and eighty, 19 080.
19. 20 208, 18 002, 2200, 19 008, 20 026.
20. half a million, one hundred thousand, six hundred thousand, quarter of a million, fifty thousand.

Example 5

Give the largest and smallest number that can be made using *all* the following digits.

a) 3, 8, 6 and 1   b) 9, 0, 1 and 9

a) Largest is 8631 : smallest is 1368
b) Largest is 9910 : smallest is 1099.

0199 should be written as 199; this only involves three digits instead of all four.

Exercise 7

Give the largest and smallest number that can be made using *all* the following digits.

1. 6 and 2	2. 7 and 8
3. 1, 3 and 4	4. 2, 4 and 1
5. 3, 5 and 0	6. 3, 5 and 2
7. 4, 9 and 3	8. 6, 8 and 1
9. 5, 3 and 5	10. 7, 6 and 0

11. 4, 1, 9 and 7	12. 4, 3, 6 and 5
13. 5, 1, and 7	14. 2, 8, 1 and 5
15. 3, 5, 0 and 2	16. 6, 3, 3 and 6
17. 4, 6, 4 and 0	18. 9, 7, 0 and 0
19. 7, 1, 2 and 8	20. 2, 0, 0 and 2

21. 4, 3, 1, 6 and 2	22. 5, 1, 7, 3 and 6
23. 5, 2, 2, 0 and 5	24. 7, 3, 3, 3 and 7
25. 6, 9, 6, 9 and 6	26. 7, 7, 0, 0 and 7
27. 1, 3, 2, 6, 5, 6 and 8	28. 2, 0, 0, 3, 0, 4 and 7
29. 3, 4, 4, 6, 3 and 5	30. 4, 0, 0, 0, 4 and 0

You can multiply a number by 10 by moving each figure one place to the left and putting zero in the empty units space.

So, a) 3 X 10 = 3 tens and 0 units = 30

b) 406 X 10 = 4060

Th	H	T	U		Th	H	T	U
	4	0	6		4	0	6	0

Exercise 8

Multiply each of these numbers by 10.

1. 2	2. 7	3. 6	4. 9
5. 15	6. 19	7. 10	8. 24
9. 30	10. 45		

11. 42	12. 53	13. 67	14, 70
15. 80	16. 124	17. 253	18. 350
19. 276	20. 484		

21. 762	22. 802	23. 780	24. 600
25. 2317	26. 3180	27. 4200	28. 5010
29. 7000	30. 6401		

31. 8462	32. 7070	33. 4000
34. 12 040	35. 13 675	36. 24 600
37. 35 000	38. 214 160	39. 348 000
40. 700 000		

You can divide a number by 10 by moving each figure one place to the right; the units figure becomes the remainder.

So, a) 50 ÷ 10 = 5 with a remainder of 0.
     i.e. 5

b) 632 ÷ 10 = 63 with a remainder of 2.
     i.e. 63 r 2

Exercise 9

Divide each of these numbers by 10.

1. 20	2. 70	3. 60	4. 90
5. 22	6. 43	7. 84	8. 79
9. 61	10. 55		

11. 150	12. 260	13. 720	14. 310
15. 600	16. 112	17. 306	18. 709
19. 342	20. 729		

21. 1250	22. 4000	23. 6800
24. 5926	25. 6543	26. 9889
27. 47 600	28. 57 100	29. 496 502
30. 4900 000		

To multiply by 100, move each figure two places to the left, and put noughts in the empty tens and units spaces.

So, a) 3 × 100 = 300

b) 406 × 100 = 40 600

Exercise 10

Multiply each of these numbers by 100.

1. 3	**2.** 9	**3.** 13	**4.** 16
5. 10	**6.** 25	**7.** 51	**8.** 78
9. 30	**10.** 60		

11. 124	**12.** 237	**13.** 519	**14.** 708
15. 630	**16.** 810	**17.** 400	**18.** 900
19. 100	**20.** 999		

21. 476	**22.** 5610	**23.** 4900	**24.** 0
25. 8960	**26.** 12 300	**27.** 29 600	
28. 47 000	**29.** 5940	**30.** 80 000	

To divide by 100, move each figure two places to the right.

So, a) 500 ÷ 100 = 5

b) 7263 ÷ 100 = 72 r 63

Exercise 11

Divide each of these numbers by 100.

1. 200	**2.** 600	**3.** 800	**4.** 850
5. 853	**6.** 764	**7.** 704	**8.** 502
9. 3200	**10.** 9700		

11. 9710	**12.** 4680	**13.** 4683	**14.** 5162
15. 9375	**16.** 4118	**17.** 1384	**18.** 3725
19. 3705	**20.** 5107		

21. 5007	**22.** 2008	**23.** 2030	**24.** 8070
25. 11 000	**26.** 76 000	**27.** 84 408	**28.** 96 069
29. 154 000		**30.** 3 046 000	

Exercise 12

Multiply each of these numbers by 1000.

1. 4	**2.** 15	**3.** 34	**4.** 120
5. 204	**6.** 841	**7.** 60	**8.** 400

Divide each of these numbers by 1000.

9. 4000	**10.** 17 000	**11.** 85 000	**12.** 8432
13. 26 062	**14.** 38 006	**15.** 425 040	**16.** 836

Multiply each of these numbers by 10 000

17. 6	**18.** 28	**19.** 70	**20.** 620
21. 900	**22.** 201	**23.** 2260	**24.** 1000

Divide each of these numbers by 10 000

25. 170 000	**26.** 840 000	**27.** 6000 000
28. 48 700	**29.** 740 600	**30.** 1250

Example 6

a) A wallpaper shop received 4 boxes of wallpaper. If each box contained 10 rolls, how many rolls of wallpaper did the shop receive?

b) The next day, the shop ordered 28 rolls of wallpaper.
 i) How many boxes will be delivered?
 ii) How many rolls will be in the last box?

a) Number of rolls = 4 × 10
                         = 40

b) 28 ÷ 10 = 2 r 8

 i) Number of boxes = 3
    i.e. 2 full and 1 partly full.

 ii) Number of rolls in last box = 8

Exercise 13

1. There are 10 boys at Tom's birthday party. Tom bakes 6 cakes for each person. How many cakes does he bake?

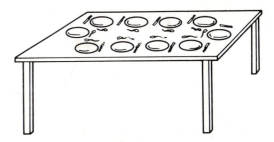

2. A publisher puts 10 copies of a book into a packet. A bookshop orders 70 copies of the book. How many packets will the bookshop receive?

3. A small car factory produces 12 cars each day. How many cars will be produced in 10 days?

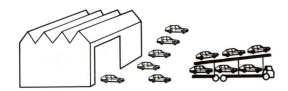

4. A farmer has 23 pens with 10 sheep in each pen. How many sheep are in the pens altogether?

5. A box of shirts contains 10 shirts. A shop receives 210 shirts. How many boxes were the shirts in?

6. Pupils in a class each use 10 maths jotters per year. How many jotters are needed for this class of 24 pupils for a year?

7. A teacher has 125 sheets of paper to share out amongst 10 pupils.
   a) How many sheets does each pupil get?
   b) How many sheets does the teacher have left over?

8. A bricklayer lays 75 concrete blocks per hour. How many will he lay in 10 hours?

9. A multi-storey block of flats has 10 flats on each storey except the top storey which has less. There are 126 flats altogether.
   a) How many storeys are there?
   b) How many flats are there in the top storey?

10. Coloured pencils are packed in boxes of ten. How many boxes are needed for 1500 pencils?

11. In an inter-school competition, there are 90 pupils. If there are 10 pupils from each school, how many schools are represented?

12. In a supermarket, apples are sold in packs of four. How many apples are needed for one hundred packs?

13. A hotel lounge is covered with carpet tiles. There are 44 rows of tiles with 100 tiles in each row. How many tiles are on the lounge floor?

14. A container lorry can carry 100 large boxes. A factory has 2500 boxes to be taken to the docks. How many container lorries will be needed to take the boxes to the docks?

15. A discount store was supplied with 1900 televisions. It sold 100 of them each week. How many weeks did the supply last?

16. A superstore orders tins of soup in bulk. It receives 100 boxes. If each box contains 48 tins, how many tins were ordered?

17. A coal merchant has only 418 bags of coal in his stock which he has to share out among 100 customers.
   a) How many bags can he supply to each customer if they all get the same amount?
   b) How many bags will he have left over?

18. A forest nursery has 14 640 young spruce trees. They are all lifted and packed in bundles of 100.
   a) How many bundles will there be?
   b) How many trees will be left over?

1.2   Addition and subtraction

Example 1

Add the following to find the 'odd answer out'.

a) $6 + 8 + 4 + 2$ b) $7 + 2 + 9 + 3$
c) $6 + 4 + 5 + 6$ d) $8 + 1 + 5 + 7$

a)	b)	c)	d)
6	7	6	8
8	2	4	1
4	9	5	5
+ 2	+ 3	+ 6	+ 7
20	21	21	21

So (a) has the 'odd answer out' because its answer is 20.

Exercise 14

Add the following to find the 'odd answer out'.

1.
a)	b)	c)	d)
2	7	8	4
5	2	1	3
3	3	6	7
+ 8	+ 6	+ 4	+ 4

2.
a)	b)	c)	d)
7	6	8	6
8	8	4	9
9	5	5	4
+ 3	+ 7	+ 9	+ 7

3. a) $9 + 6 + 7 + 7$ b) $8 + 5 + 6 + 9$
   c) $7 + 9 + 4 + 8$ d) $8 + 8 + 5 + 7$

4. a) $8 + 9 + 7 + 6$ b) $9 + 7 + 9 + 5$
   c) $9 + 8 + 8 + 5$ d) $7 + 7 + 8 + 9$

5. a) 21   b) 23   c) 22   d) 25
       13   11   10   11
       10   12   15   10
     + 14   + 13   + 11   + 12
     ────   ────   ────   ────

6. a) 16   b) 17   c) 15   d) 18
       15   12   13   11
       13   12   13   12
     + 11   + 13   + 14   + 14
     ────   ────   ────   ────

7. a) $15 + 13 + 17 + 11$ b) $14 + 12 + 16 + 15$
   c) $16 + 14 + 14 + 13$ d) $13 + 12 + 19 + 13$

8. a) $18 + 13 + 22 + 24$ b) $17 + 15 + 11 + 34$
   c) $13 + 27 + 11 + 26$ d) $32 + 14 + 15 + 15$

9. a) 17   b) 14   c)   3   d)   5
        4   7   13   18
       16   15   15   12
     + 2   + 3   + 7   + 4
     ────   ────   ────   ────

10. a) 25   b) 12   c)   3   d)   5
         7   8   11   25
        11   24   27   12
      + 4   + 3   + 6   + 6
      ────   ────   ────   ────

11. a) 15   b) 13   c)   9   d)   3
         6   8   11   8
         4   5   6   12
      + 2   + 2   + 1   + 4
      ────   ────   ────   ────

12. a) $11 + 8 + 13 + 9$ b) $15 + 4 + 17 + 5$
    c) $9 + 15 + 14 + 4$ d) $7 + 14 + 16 + 4$

13. a) $35 + 3 + 26 + 8$ b) $9 + 45 + 12 + 6$
    c) $29 + 7 + 33 + 4$ d) $3 + 41 + 9 + 19$

14. a) $37 + 9 + 18 + 9$ b) $27 + 8 + 29 + 8$
    c) $29 + 6 + 28 + 9$ d) $19 + 9 + 36 + 8$

15. a) $27 + 8 + 17 + 9$ b) $6 + 19 + 19 + 18$
    c) $19 + 9 + 28 + 5$ d) $8 + 16 + 18 + 19$

16. a)   234   b)   127   c)   15
         116   47   256
       + 28   + 205   + 107
       ─────   ─────   ─────

17. a) $167 + 45 + 352$ **18.** a) $326 + 145 + 44$
    b) $241 + 187 + 36$ b) $275 + 36 + 214$
    c) $154 + 82 + 328$ c) $33 + 255 + 227$

19. a)   232   b)   42   c)   61
          20   251   43
       + 72   + 31   + 230
       ─────   ─────   ─────

20. a) $46 + 213 + 36$ **21.** a) $48 + 63 + 245$
    b) $230 + 39 + 27$ b) $27 + 306 + 23$
    c) $64 + 209 + 23$ c) $282 + 37 + 38$

22. a)   612   b)   430   c)   532
         121   323   342
       + 244   + 234   + 113
       ─────   ─────   ─────

23. a) $224 + 523 + 131$
    b) $635 + 112 + 132$
    c) $353 + 104 + 422$

24. a) $155 + 424 + 147$
    b) $263 + 225 + 238$
    c) $324 + 153 + 248$

25. a) $338 + 413 + 234$
    b) $527 + 243 + 115$
    c) $213 + 216 + 456$

26. a) $55 + 20 + 31 + 211$
    b) $43 + 21 + 241 + 12$
    c) $31 + 222 + 24 + 50$

27. a) $57 + 12 + 303 + 211$
    b) $144 + 401 + 26 + 13$
    c) $22 + 214 + 333 + 15$

28. a) $255 + 324 + 221 + 56$
    b) $363 + 346 + 12 + 145$
    c) $37 + 440 + 122 + 257$

29. a) $245 + 231 + 102 + 254$
    b) $113 + 156 + 341 + 222$
    c) $127 + 230 + 251 + 124$

30. a) $166 + 341 + 202 + 232$
    b) $275 + 330 + 122 + 114$
    c) $284 + 311 + 133 + 213$

Example 2

Subtract the following to find the 'odd answer out'.

a) $28 - 12$ b) $63 - 47$
c) $95 - 79$ d) $90 - 64$

a)	28	b)	63	c)	95	d)	90
	-12		-47		-79		-64
	16		16		16		26

So d) is the 'odd answer out' because its answer is 26.

Exercise 15

Subtract the following to find the 'odd answer out'.

1. a) 66   b) 49   c) 77   d) 55
    -41 -23 -52 -30

2. a) 57   b) 88   c) 65   d) 79
    -23 -55 -32 -46

3. a) $58 - 16$ **4.** a) $97 - 43$ **5.** a) $68 - 12$
b) $84 - 41$ b) $74 - 20$ b) $97 - 51$
c) $75 - 33$ c) $89 - 35$ c) $86 - 40$
d) $97 - 55$ d) $66 - 11$ d) $79 - 33$

6. a) $96 - 33$ **7.** a) $78 - 26$ **8.** a) $96 - 51$
b) $75 - 11$ b) $94 - 43$ b) $49 - 4$
c) $87 - 24$ c) $59 - 7$ c) $75 - 40$
d) $69 - 6$ d) $66 - 14$ d) $57 - 12$

9. a) $39 - 3$ **10.** a) $79 - 35$ **11.** a) $72 - 37$
b) $67 - 31$ b) $54 - 20$ b) $94 - 59$
c) $46 - 10$ c) $86 - 52$ c) $63 - 28$
d) $98 - 52$ d) $97 - 63$ d) $81 - 45$

12. a) $75 - 28$ **13.** a) $44 - 28$ **14.** a) $62 - 34$
b) $91 - 44$ b) $63 - 46$ b) $45 - 16$
c) $63 - 15$ c) $71 - 55$ c) $86 - 57$
d) $86 - 39$ d) $55 - 39$ d) $74 - 45$

15. a) $64 - 25$ **16.** a) $51 - 45$ **17.** a) $52 - 25$
b) $87 - 49$ b) $93 - 87$ b) $83 - 57$
c) $75 - 37$ c) $74 - 69$ c) $45 - 18$
d) $90 - 52$ d) $80 - 74$ d) $96 - 69$

18. a) $62 - 13$ **19.** a) $93 - 37$ **20.** a) $62 - 24$
b) $85 - 37$ b) $75 - 29$ b) $94 - 56$
c) $73 - 25$ c) $62 - 16$ c) $97 - 49$
d) $90 - 42$ d) $55 - 9$ d) $46 - 8$

Example 3

Subtract to find the difference between the following pairs of numbers and so find the 'odd answer out'.

a) 676 and 394   b) 309 and 27
c) 584 and 292

a)	676	b)	309	c)	584
	-394		-27		-292
	282		282		292

So (c) has the 'odd answer out' because its answer is 292.

Exercise 16

Subtract to find the difference between the following pairs of numbers and so find the 'odd answer out'.

1. a) 797 and 352   **2.** a) 876 and 252
b) 856 and 421   b) 968 and 344
c) 669 and 234   c) 747 and 133

3. a) 586 and 214   **4.** a) 797 and 541
b) 794 and 432   b) 376 and 130
c) 678 and 306   c) 658 and 412

5. a) 897 and 384   **6.** a) 788 and 147
b) 759 and 236   b) 996 and 354
c) 983 and 460   c) 849 and 208

7. a) 895 and 432   **8.** a) 598 and 253
b) 668 and 205   b) 976 and 621
c) 789 and 327   c) 665 and 320

9. a) 397 and 74   **10.** a) 594 and 51
b) 365 and 52   b) 579 and 37
c) 386 and 63   c) 585 and 43

11. a) 729 and 243   **12.** a) 947 and 383
b) 857 and 381   b) 826 and 262
c) 648 and 162   c) 769 and 195

13. a) 615 and 253   **14.** a) 492 and 237
b) 538 and 186   b) 664 and 419
c) 807 and 445   c) 573 and 328

15. a) 381 and 257   **16.** a) 373 and 27
b) 550 and 426   b) 361 and 16
c) 272 and 138   c) 384 and 39

17. a) 422 and 143   **18.** a) 623 and 237
b) 614 and 325   b) 861 and 485
c) 541 and 262   c) 744 and 368

19. a) 614 and 31   **20.** a) 543 and 75
b) 638 and 54   b) 505 and 38
c) 606 and 23   c) 514 and 46

Example 4

Farmer Jones has 22 cattle in one field and 17 in another field. How many cattle has he in the two fields altogether?

$$\text{Number of cattle} = 22 + 17$$
$$= 39$$

Example 5

The local factory employs 112 people. One Monday there were only 98 workers in the factory. How many were absent on that Monday?

$$\text{Number of workers absent} = 112 - 98$$
$$= 14$$

Exercise 17

1. A school bus has 23 passengers. If six more get on, how many passengers are on the bus now?

2. There are 14 girls and 12 boys in a class. How many pupils are there in the class altogether?
3. Mark has 16 sweets. If he eats 7 of them, how many sweets has he left?
4. There were 41 passengers on a bus. If 17 people got off, how many passengers were left on the bus?
5. Mr Smith buys 24 eggs on Friday. Over the weekend, he uses 9 eggs. How many eggs has he left?

6. Jane has 9 records and Susan has 16 records. How many records have they altogether?

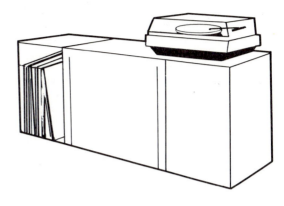

7. George takes 7 steps from his front gate to his front door. He takes another 28 steps from the front door to the back door. How many steps is it from George's front gate to his back door?

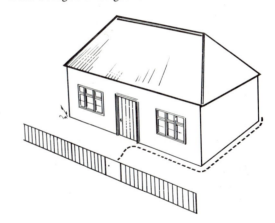

8. On Saturday morning 54 people paid to go swimming and on Saturday afternoon 68 people paid to go swimming. What is the total number of people who paid to go swimming on Saturday?
9. Patricia baked 16 rock cakes and 22 queen cakes. How many cakes did she bake altogether?
10. A school hall has seats for 450 people. At a concert there were 374 people. How many empty seats were there?
11. There are 28 pupils in a class. If 16 are girls, how many are boys?
12. The school cricket team needs 75 runs to win. Trevor scores 39 runs. How many runs must the rest of the team score?
13. Beth has a magazine collection of 36 Mandys and Jackies. If she has 21 Jackies, how many Mandys has she?

14. Peter has 12 coloured pencils and 18 felt pens. How many pens and pencils has he altogether?

15. When playing cricket, Henry scored 36 runs off John's bowling and 19 runs off Fred's bowling before he was out. How many runs did Henry score?

16. Sushma got 26 marks in her first test and 18 marks in her second test. How many marks did she get in the two tests?

17. A cat lover bought a box of 48 tins of cat food on Tuesday. By Friday her cats had eaten 19 tins. How many tins were left?

18. A football team scored 53 goals in a season. If they scored 29 goals in home games, how many did they score in away games?

19. A shop receives 85 evening papers every night. On Wednesday evening it sold 68 papers. How many evening papers were left unsold?

20. A daily newspaper has 28 pages. On Thursday it produces a 12-page supplement. How many pages are published on Thursday?

21. A gardener picked 4 cauliflowers in the first week of September, 7 in the second and 5 in the third week. If she did not pick any more, how many cauliflowers did she pick in September?

22. On a school trip there were 56 pupils in the first bus and 39 pupils in the second bus. How many pupils went on the trip?

23. There are 285 people who want to fly on the Glasgow to London shuttle. If the first plane carries 168 passengers, how many passengers will be on the second plane?

24. In one season Liverpool scored 84 goals and lost 46 goals. How many goals were scored in all Liverpool's matches?

25. A factory worker packed 187 boxes on Monday and 196 boxes on Tuesday. What is the total number of boxes packed by the factory worker on Monday and Tuesday?

26. In the first innings of a test match England scored 428 runs and Australia scored 379 runs. How big a lead did England have?

27. On Friday a superstore received 430 loaves and sold 387. How many loaves were left on Friday night?

28. At the end of the session 328 pupils left Hopwood High School. At the beginning of the next session 284 new pupils arrived. By how much was the school role at Hopwood reduced?

29. A village hall used 842 units of electricity in the first quarter of the year, 546 in the second quarter, 485 in the third quarter and 692 in the last quarter. How many units of electricity were used in the whole year?

30. In an archery competition Sarah fired 100 arrows. If 64 hit the target, how many missed the target?

31. On Thursday a baker made 240 white loaves, 185 brown loaves and 76 wholemeal loaves. How many loaves did the baker make on Thursday?

32. A boutique bought 125 dresses. After a month the manager had a sale of the last 19 dresses. How many dresses were sold before the sale?

33. On a special flight to a European cup tie, there were 18 players, 8 officials, 13 pressmen and 45 supporters. How many passengers were on the plane?

34. In an election 22 496 people voted for the Conservative candidate and 18 962 people voted for the Alliance candidate. How many more votes did the Conservative candidate get?

35. A delivery girl took the lift up to the 17th floor of a multi-storey block to deliver a parcel. She then walked down 6 floors for her second delivery. On which floor was she when she made the second delivery?

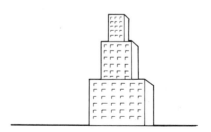

36. At a football match there were 12 840 adults and 6976 children. What was the total attendance?

37. A farmer bought 462 sheep at Lairg, 594 sheep at St Boswells and 643 sheep at Lanark. How many sheep did he buy altogether?

38. Before laying a gas pipeline, a company had 4850 pipes at one depot, 2395 at a second depot and 5642 at a third depot. How many pipes were there in the three depots?

39. A large car park holds 532 cars. At one o'clock there were 455 cars in the car park. At two o'clock the car park was full. How many cars must have entered the car park between one o'clock and two o'clock?

40. A train left London with 640 passengers, all going to Liverpool or Manchester. The train was split at Crewe and 273 passengers were on the Liverpool section. How many were on the Manchester section of the train?

Example 6

Find the sum of:

a) 406, 23, 17, 181, 109.

b) Eighty-four, six hundred, two hundred and twenty-two, nine.

```
a)    406          b)     84
       23                600
       17                222
      181              +   9
    + 109               ___
    _____               915
      736               ___
    _____
```

Exercise 18

In each of the following questions find which list of numbers has a different sum from the other two.

1. a) 352, 41, 24, 216, 323.
b) 507, 263, 50, 21, 125.
c) 240, 401, 208, 54, 63.

2. a) 305, 23, 51, 40, 203.
b) 32, 300, 207, 10, 73.
c) 42, 23, 31, 406, 110.

3. a) 105, 3, 94, 550, 123.
b) 81, 344, 302, 134, 4.
c) 6, 470, 200, 152, 37.

4. a) 365, 81, 4, 2, 260.
b) 482, 180, 5, 1, 54.
c) 7, 261, 90, 352, 2.

5. a) 115, 58, 42, 55, 3.
b) 41, 36, 8, 122, 56.
c) 52, 154, 33, 6, 28.

6. a) Eighty-seven, four hundred and one, two hundred and ninety, four.
b) Three hundred and twenty-seven, ninety, five, three hundred and seventy.
c) Six, eighty-two, one hundred and ninety-four, five hundred.

7. a) Fifty-six, forty-two, two hundred and thirty, seven.
b) Two hundred and four, six, fifty, seventy-five.
c) Nine, ninety-four, two hundred, forty-two.

8. a) Five hundred and seventy, two hundred and forty-one, five, three.
b) Six, four hundred and eighty-one, three hundred and forty, two.
c) Six hundred and fifty, five, four, one hundred and sixty.

9. a) Two hundred, four hundred and four, three hundred and thirty-eight, fifty.
b) One hundred and eleven, two hundred and six, sixty-five, six hundred.
c) Thirty, five hundred and twenty, one hundred and four, three hundred and twenty-eight.

10. a) Three hundred and five, ninety-nine, fifty, one hundred and sixty-seven.
b) Ninety, eighty-eight, two hundred and twenty-six, two hundred and seven.
c) One hundred and eighteen, forty, seventy-five, three hundred and eighty-eight.

Example 7

By adding and subtracting, work out the following.

a) $76 + 82 - 69$ b) $9 - 253 + 607$

```
a)      76      b) Rearrange as follows:
     +  82           9 + 607 - 253
       ___
       158            9          616
     -  69         + 607       - 253
       ___          ____        ____
        89           616         363
       ___          ____        ____
```

Exercise 19

Find the 'odd answer out' for the following:

1. a) $288 + 154 - 317$
   b) $396 + 178 - 439$
   c) $197 + 186 - 258$

2. a) $38 + 307 - 182$
   b) $508 + 29 - 384$
   c) $19 + 425 - 291$

3. a) $382 + 275 - 39$
   b) $191 + 485 - 48$
   c) $272 + 363 - 17$

4. a) $87 + 555 - 176$
   b) $658 + 73 - 265$
   c) $57 + 893 - 494$

5. a) $7 + 348 - 78$
   b) $9 + 324 - 46$
   c) $6 + 368 - 87$

6. a) $25 - 41 + 58$
   b) $18 - 49 + 74$
   c) $36 - 53 + 59$

7. a) $134 - 196 + 225$
   b) $190 - 319 + 292$
   c) $248 - 262 + 167$

8. a) $57 - 148 + 235$
   b) $81 - 282 + 355$
   c) $72 - 109 + 191$

9. a) $8 - 29 + 135$
   b) $5 - 68 + 187$
   c) $7 - 80 + 197$

10. a) $58 - 76 + 181$
    b) $30 - 42 + 185$
    c) $19 - 47 + 191$

Example 8

In a competition, five balls are rolled into numbered slots. If four balls have been rolled as shown, what is a) the total score, b) the score that the fifth ball must make to win i) a 'free go', ii) a prize?

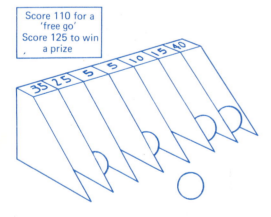

Score 110 for a 'free go'
Score 125 to win a prize

a) Total score $= 25 + 5 + 15 + 40 = 85$

b) To win a 'free go' the fifth ball must score,
$110 - 85 = 25$

To win a prize the fifth ball must score,
$125 - 85 = 40$

Exercise 20

1. John had 12 marbles. He lost 4 to Jim and won 3 from Chris. How many marbles has John now?

2. The milkman uses a crate containing 20 bottles to deliver milk to Short Street.
   How many bottles will he have left when he gets to the end of the street?

MILK ORDERS FOR SHORT STREET
MRS JONES, No. 1   4 BOTTLES
MR ADAMS, No. 2   2 BOTTLES
MRS BUTLER, No. 3   1 BOTTLE
MISS HAYNES, No. 4 NONE TODAY.
MRS ASHURST, No. 5   3 BOTTLES
MR BIGGS, No. 6   1 BOTTLE

3. In a class of 28 pupils, 14 walk to school, 5 cycle to school and the rest come by bus. How many come by bus?

4. Jane, Elizabeth, and Donna arrange a party. Jane invites 12 friends, Elizabeth invites 7 different friends and Donna invites 5 other friends.
   a) How many were invited to the party?
   b) If 4 people could not come, how many were at the party?

5. A farmer has 84 rows of potatoes to lift. On Wednesday he lifts 25 rows. On Thursday he lifts 31 rows and on Friday he lifts the rest. How many rows does he lift on Friday?

6. Peter and William compete in an archery contest. Look at their scores below.

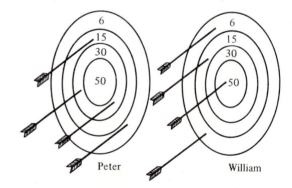

Peter   William

a) How many points did Peter score?
b) How many points did William score?
c) Who has won the contest and by how many points?

7. There were 32 people on a bus when it left Perth. At Pitlochry, 14 passengers got on, and 21 got off at Aviemore. How many people were left on the bus when it left Aviemore?

8. There are 92 buses in a fleet. On Monday morning 9 buses were off the road with mechanical trouble, 1 was off with accident damage and 2 were off after being vandalised. How many buses could be used on Monday morning?

9. At Willow Bank School there are 455 girls and 428 boys. How many pupils are there altogether? How many more girls are there than boys?

10. There are 746 steps to the top of a tall monument. Diane walked up 235 steps before taking a rest. In the next stage, she climbed 204 steps. In the third stage, she walked up another 187 steps. How many steps has she still to climb?

11. One Monday morning a supermarket had 420 packets of washing powder. During the week it sold 396 packets and received delivery of 288 packets. How many packets had it at the end of the week?

12. In a self-service restaurant there was a queue of 32 people. In the next 5 minutes, 18 people were served and another 26 joined the queue.

How many people were now in the queue?

13. One month a garage sold 18 new cars, and accepted 15 cars in part-exchange. It also sold 34 second-hand cars and accepted 22 cars in part-exchange. How many fewer cars had the garage at the end of the month?

14. There were 16 850 spectators at a football match between Aberdeen and Dundee United. If 11 680 spectators supported Aberdeen and 4935 supported Dundee United, how many spectators supported neither team?

15. A gardener transplanted 96 leeks and 72 onions. If 5 onions and 7 leeks died, how many plants survived?

16. A woman buys two magazines. One has 124 pages and the other has 92 pages. The first magazine has 73 pages of advertisements, while the second has 39 pages of advertisements. Out of both magazines, how many pages did not have advertisements?

17. In a fishing competition, team A caught 7, 10, 4 and 9 fish and Team B caught 12, 2, 8 and 6 fish.
   a) Which team caught most fish?
   b) How many more fish did this team catch than the other?

18. A factory employed 152 people. For a special contract it employed an extra 39 people. At the end of the contract, the company had to make 65 people redundant. How many people were now employed in the factory?

19. Fatty Tucker ate five buns on Monday. On Tuesday he ate two more buns than on Monday. On Wednesday he ate two more than on Tuesday, and so on.
   a) How many buns did Fatty eat on Friday?
   b) How many buns did he eat in the five days from Monday to Friday?

20. A cigarette smoker decides to give up the habit.

Each day she is going to smoke two less cigarettes than the day before. On Sunday 1st January, she smokes 20 cigarettes.
   a) What is the first day she will smoke no cigarettes?
   b) How many cigarettes will she smoke in January?

1.3   Number sets

The *whole* numbers are 0, 1, 2, 3, 4 . . .
An *even* number is obtained when a whole number is multiplied by 2.
The even numbers are 0, 2, 4, 6, 8 . . .
An *odd* number is obtained when 1 is added to an even number.
The odd numbers are 1, 3, 5, 7, 9 . . .

Exercise 21

1. Here are some football results.

Arsenal	4	Nottingham Forest	1
Everton	1	Watford	0
Luton Town	3	Southampton	1
Manchester United	2	Liverpool	1

   a) Which teams scored an even number of goals?
   b) Which teams scored an odd number of goals?

2. List the next five even numbers starting from:
   a) 4   b) 16   c) 32   d) 88   e) 100

3. List the next five odd numbers starting from:
   a) 5   b) 13   c) 31   d) 69   e) 117

4. Six children have each thrown two dice. Look at their total scores below.

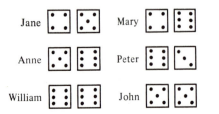

   a) Whose scores are even numbers?
   b) Whose scores are odd numbers?

5. Sally and Emma scored 8 with two dice. Sally's dice were both odd, and Emma's dice were both even.

   a) Which numbers could be on Sally's dice?
   b) Which numbers could be on Emma's dice?

6. Emma now throws 7 with two dice. Which numbers could be on her dice?

A *square* number is any whole number that can be represented by counters arranged in a square.

Example 1

Draw and write down the first three square numbers after nought.

A square number is found by multiplying any whole number by itself.
Because $0 \times 0 = 0$, 0 is also a square number.

A *rectangular* number is any whole number that can be represented by counters arranged in a rectangle.
A proper rectangular number has at least two rows and two columns.

Example 2

Draw rectangular numbers 6, 8 and 15.

A *triangular* number is any whole number that can be represented by counters arranged in a triangle.

Example 3

Draw and write down the first three triangular numbers.

Exercise 22

1. Look at the numbers on the signposts A, B and C.

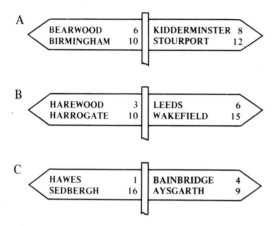

a) On which signpost are *all* the numbers square?
b) On which signpost are *all* the numbers rectangular?
c) On which signpost are *all* the numbers triangular?

2. Draw and write down
a) the first ten square numbers,
b) the first ten triangular numbers.

3. State whether the following numbers are square (S), proper rectangular (R), triangular (T) or none of these (N).
For example, 15 is (R, T); 17 is (N).
a) 12   b) 14   c) 16   d) 21   e) 7
f) 18   g) 19   h) 25   i) 28   j) 36

4. Can you find
a) any odd numbers which are also square numbers?
b) any numbers which are both proper rectangular and odd?
c) any even numbers which are not proper rectangular numbers?
Give examples if you can.

5. Find the sum of
a) the first three odd numbers
b) the first four odd numbers
c) the first five odd numbers
d) the first ten odd numbers
e) the first thirty odd numbers

6. Look at the ten triangular numbers you found in question 2b.
Add together
a) the first and second
b) the second and third
c) the third and fourth
d) the fourth and fifth
e) the fifth and sixth
f) The numbers in the above answers are all of the same kind. What are they?

A *prime* number is any whole number which is not a square number or a proper rectangular number.
Any whole number which is only divisible by itself or by 1 is therefore a prime number.

The first prime numbers are 2, 3, 5, 7 and 11.

Exercise 23

1. Look at the four buses A, B, C and D.

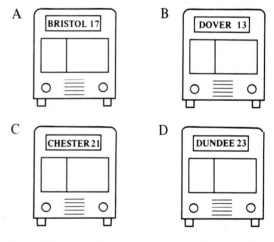

One of the buses is not displaying a prime number. Which one is it?

2. List all the prime numbers between 1 and 30.

3. Which of the following are prime numbers?
a) 31   b) 33   c) 37   d) 35   e) 49   f) 43
g) 51   h) 41   i) 53   j) 57   k) 63   l) 61

A sequence is a set of numbers in which each number is related to the other by a rule.

Example 4

a) 1, 4, 7, 10 . . . is a sequence in which each term is three more than the one before it.
b) 1, 4, 16, 64 . . . is a sequence in which each term is four times the one before it.

Exercise 24

1. Find the heights of the next two arches of the viaduct below.

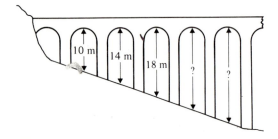

2. Find the next five terms of the sequences.
   a) 3, 4, 5, 6 . . .   b) 11, 12, 13, 14 . . .
   c) 71, 70, 69, 68 . . . d) 105, 104, 103, 102 . . .
   e) 6, 8, 10, 12 . . .   f) 46, 44, 42, 40 . . .
   g) 6, 9, 12, 15 . . .   h) 45, 42, 39, 36 . . .
   i) 60, 65, 70, 75 . . .   j) 64, 60, 56, 52 . . .
   k) 6, 12, 18, 24 . . .   l) 56, 49, 42, 35 . . .
   m) 0, 8, 16, 24 . . .   n) 81, 72, 63, 54 . . .

3. Find the next four terms of the sequences.
   a) 3, 5, 7, 9 . . .   b) 57, 55, 53, 51 . . .
   c) 1, 4, 7, 10 . . .   d) 43, 40, 37, 34 . . .
   e) 3, 7, 11, 15 . . .   f) 62, 58, 54, 50 . . .
   g) 17, 23, 29, 35 . . .   h) 53, 48, 43, 38 . . .
   i) 2, 11, 20, 29 . . .   j) 67, 59, 51, 43 . . .

4. In each of the following, state which term does not fit. Write out the correct sequence.
   a) 14, 16, 19, 20, 22   b) 3, 6, 9, 13, 15
   c) 16, 20, 24, 30, 32   d) 6, 14, 18, 24, 30
   e) 72, 64, 54, 48, 40   f) 32, 29, 26, 23, 21
   g) 60, 56, 51, 46, 41   h) 18, 22, 25, 30, 34

5. Find the next five terms of the sequences and state the rule in each case.
   a) 2, 4, 6, 8 . . .   b) 3, 6, 9, 12 . . .
   c) 12, 24, 36, 48 . . .   d) 56, 49, 42, 35 . . .
   e) 8, 13, 18, 23 . . .   f) 5, 11, 17, 23 . . .
   g) 40, 36, 32, 28 . . .   h) 90, 82, 74, 66 . . .

6. When a seed is planted, it develops 1 root in the first week. Every week after that, each root develops 3 new roots. How many new roots grow in the fourth week?

seed	1 week	2 weeks	3 weeks	4 weeks

        1 new root   3 new roots   9 new roots   ?

7. Find the next three terms of the sequences and state the rule in each case.
   a) 2, 4, 8, 16 . . .   b) 3, 9, 27, 81 . . .
   c) 1, 4, 16, 64 . . .   d) 1, 5, 25, 125 . . .
   e) 1, 10, 100 . . .   f) 512, 256, 128 . . .
   g) 243, 81, 27 . . .   h) 200 000, 20 000, 2000
   i) 2, 10, 50 . . .   j) 2, 6, 18 . . .

8. In each of the following, state which term is the odd one out. Write out the correct sequence.
   a) 2, 4, 6, 9, 10   b) 3, 5, 7, 9, 10
   c) 4, 8, 12, 14, 20   d) 100, 90, 85, 70, 60
   e) 90, 81, 72, 64, 54   f) 55, 49, 42, 35, 28
   g) 1, 3, 4, 8, 16   h) 1, 4, 6, 16, 25
   i) 100, 81, 64, 50, 36   j) 2, 3, 5, 7, 11, 15, 17

9. Find the next three terms of the sequences.
   a) 1, 4, 9, 16 . . .   b) 1, 3, 6, 10 . . .
   c) 1, 8, 27, 64 . . .   d) 2, 3, 5, 7, 11, 13, . . .
   e) 8, 18, 32, 50 . . .   f) 0, 2, 5, 9 . . .
   g) 99, 80, 63, 48 . . .   h) 6, 12, 20, 30 . . .
   i) 1, 2, 3, 5, 8 . . .   j) 1, 3, 4, 7, 11 . . .
   k) 2, 5, 7, 12, 19 . . . l) 26, 16, 10, 6, 4 . . .

10. Find the next two terms of the sequences in three (or more) different ways.
    a) 2, 4 . . .   b) 1, 2 . . .
    c) 1, 4 . . .   d) 2, 3 . . .
    e) 2, 6 . . .   f) 3, 6 . . .
    g) 4, 16 . . .   h) 6, 12 . . .

1.4 Number displays

In a *magic square*, each number is different but the sum of each row, each column and each of the two diagonals is the same.

Example 1

16	3	2	13
5	10	11	8
9	6	7	12
4	15	14	1

Show that the number display above is a magic square.

Row 1 $16 + 3 + 2 + 13 = 34$
Row 2 $5 + 10 + 11 + 8 = 34$
Row 3 $9 + 6 + 7 + 12 = 34$
Row 4 $4 + 15 + 14 + 1 = 34$

Column 1 $16 + 5 + 9 + 4 = 34$
Column 2 $3 + 10 + 6 + 15 = 34$
Column 3 $2 + 11 + 7 + 14 = 34$
Column 4 $13 + 8 + 12 + 1 = 34$

Diagonal 1 $16 + 10 + 7 + 1 = 34$
Diagonal 2 $4 + 6 + 11 + 13 = 34$

Thus, the display is a magic square.

Exercise 25

State which of the following are *not* magic squares.

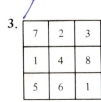

1.

4	3	8
9	5	1
2	7	6

2.

5	3	10
11	6	1
2	9	7

3.

7	2	3
1	4	8
5	6	1

4.

10	9	5
3	8	13
11	7	6

5.

4	4	7
8	5	2
3	6	6

6.

7	8	3
2	6	10
9	4	5

7.

3	11	4
7	6	5
8	1	9

8.

10	6	5
3	7	12
9	8	4

Exercise 26

Copy and complete each magic square by finding the missing numbers.

1.

		6
	5	
4	3	

2.

4	7	10
		8

3.

9		4
	6	
		3

4.

7	12	5
11		

5.

	11		
	8	12	
4	5		16
15	10	6	

6.

			6
8	15	3	12
7	16		
		14	9

7.

6		11	9
17		4	
5			
10		7	13

8.

10			11
	16	13	2
	4		
6		12	7

Investigation 1A

Magic squares

1. These are two magic squares made up from the numbers 1 to 9.

8	1	6
3	5	7
4	9	2

2	9	4
7	5	3
6	1	8

Find six more magic squares made up from these numbers.
Can you see how they are related to one another?

2. Here are two 4 × 4 magic squares using the numbers 1 to 16.

16	3	2	13
5	10	11	8
9	6	7	12
4	15	14	1

10	5	8	11
3	16	13	2
15	4	1	14
6	9	12	7

Using the numbers 1 to 16, find as many other 4 × 4 magic squares as you can.

3. Look at the 5 × 5 magic square below. Can you see how it is constructed?

17	24	1	8	15
23	5	7	14	16
4	6	13	20	22
10	12	19	21	3
11	18	25	2	9

Hint: move diagonally up to the right.

4. a) Using the technique in question 3, draw up a 3 × 3 magic square.
b) Now draw up a 7 × 7 magic square.
c) Draw up as large a magic square as you can. Each side should have an odd number of squares.

Investigation 1B

Patterns

Part of a number display is shown below.

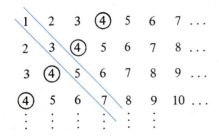

1. Name the type of number which is in the diagonal between the straight lines.
2. What kind of numbers are alongside this diagonal?
3. How many fours are in the display? What is the sum of these fours?
4. How many sevens would be in the display? What is the sum of these sevens?
5. For the above display, write down in each case the sum of all the
a) threes   b) sixes   c) eights   d) twelves
e) 20's   f) 50's   g) 200's   h) 3000's

2 Fractions

2.1 Equivalence of fractions

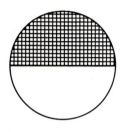
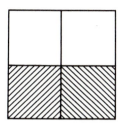
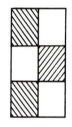
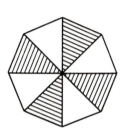

All of the above shapes have one half shaded.

$$\frac{1}{2} = \frac{2}{4} = \frac{3}{6} = \frac{4}{8}$$

Fractions having the same value are called *equivalent fractions*. Equivalent fractions can be found by two methods:

a) multiplying the top and the bottom by the same number;

e.g. i) $\frac{2}{3} = \frac{2 \times 2}{3 \times 2} = \frac{4}{6}$ ii) $\frac{3}{5} = \frac{3 \times 6}{5 \times 6} = \frac{18}{30}$

b) dividing the top and the bottom by the same number;

i) $\frac{4}{6} = \frac{4 \div 2}{6 \div 2} = \frac{2}{3}$

ii) $\frac{18}{30} = \frac{18 \div 2}{30 \div 2} = \frac{9}{15} = \frac{9 \div 3}{15 \div 3} = \frac{3}{5}$

Example 1

Find the simplest form of the fraction shaded in each of these drawings:

a)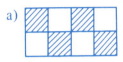

Number of parts shaded = 4
Number of equal parts   = 8
Therefore, fraction = $\frac{4}{8} = \frac{1}{2}$

b)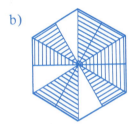

Number of parts shaded = 9
Number of equal parts   = 12
Therefore, fraction = $\frac{9}{12} = \frac{3}{4}$

Exercise 27

Find the simplest form of the fraction shaded in each of these drawings.

1. 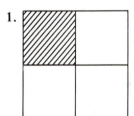   2.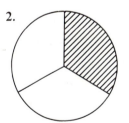

3. 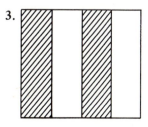   4.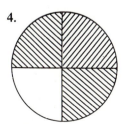

5. 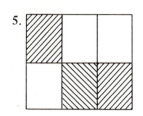   6.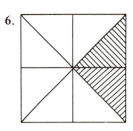

15. 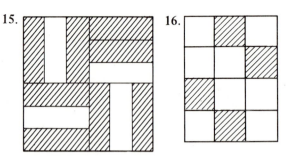 16.

7. 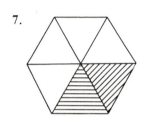   8.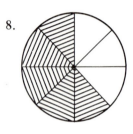

Example 2

Which of the three diagrams has a different fraction shaded?

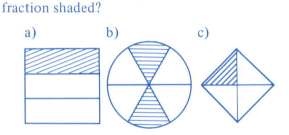

a)   b)   c)

a) 1 out of 3 parts are shaded.
   Therefore, fraction $= \frac{1}{3}$

b) 2 out of 6 parts are shaded.
   Therefore, fraction $= \frac{2}{6} = \frac{1}{3}$

c) 1 out of 4 parts are shaded.
   Therefore, fraction $= \frac{1}{4}$

Therefore c) has a different fraction shaded.

9. 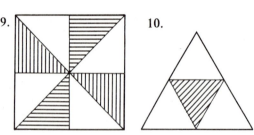   10.

Exercise 28

For each question state which of the three diagrams has a different fraction shaded.

1. a) 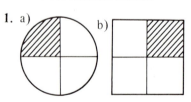 b) c)

11. 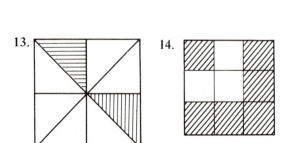   12.

2. a) 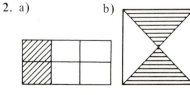 b) c)

13. 14.

3. a) b) c)

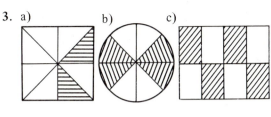

10. a) b) c)

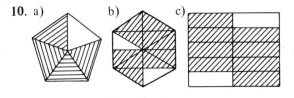

4. a) b) c)

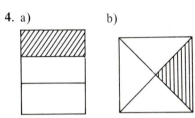

11. a) b) c)

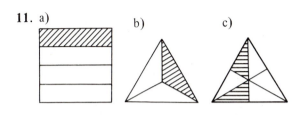

5. a) b) c)

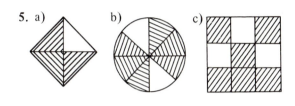

12. a) b) c)

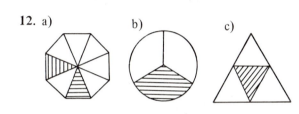

6. a) b) c)

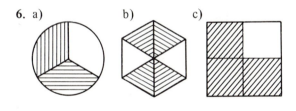

13. a) b) c)

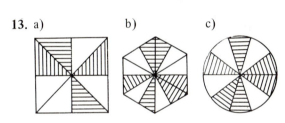

7. a) b) c)

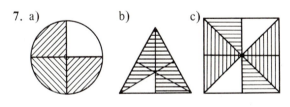

Example 3

Find which fraction is different from the other three.

a) $\frac{4}{6}$ b) $\frac{10}{15}$ c) $\frac{10}{18}$ d) $\frac{14}{21}$

In their simplest form:

a) $\frac{4}{6} = \frac{4 \div 2}{6 \div 2} = \frac{2}{3}$; b) $\frac{10}{15} = \frac{10 \div 5}{15 \div 5} = \frac{2}{3}$;

c) $\frac{10}{18} = \frac{10 \div 2}{18 \div 2} = \frac{5}{9}$; d) $\frac{14}{21} = \frac{14 \div 7}{21 \div 7} = \frac{2}{3}$.

Therefore, c) is different from the other three because it is not equivalent to $\frac{2}{3}$.

8. a) b) c)

9. a) b) c)

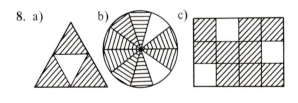

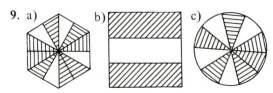

Exercise 29

For each question find which fraction is different
from the others.

1. a) $\frac{1}{2}$ b) $\frac{2}{5}$ c) $\frac{2}{4}$

2. a) $\frac{3}{5}$ b) $\frac{2}{4}$ c) $\frac{6}{10}$

3. a) $\frac{4}{6}$ b) $\frac{2}{5}$ c) $\frac{2}{3}$

4. a) $\frac{2}{8}$ b) $\frac{1}{4}$ c) $\frac{1}{2}$

5. a) $\frac{3}{5}$ b) $\frac{3}{4}$ c) $\frac{6}{8}$

6. a) $\frac{12}{16}$ b) $\frac{18}{24}$ c) $\frac{25}{30}$

7. a) $\frac{16}{24}$ b) $\frac{18}{30}$ c) $\frac{12}{18}$

8. a) $\frac{10}{12}$ b) $\frac{15}{18}$ c) $\frac{21}{24}$

9. a) $\frac{10}{25}$ b) $\frac{4}{10}$ c) $\frac{15}{40}$

10. a) $\frac{12}{36}$ b) $\frac{8}{32}$ c) $\frac{7}{28}$

11. a) $\frac{3}{15}$ b) $\frac{7}{35}$ c) $\frac{5}{20}$

12. a) $\frac{4}{24}$ b) $\frac{6}{30}$ c) $\frac{7}{42}$

13. a) $\frac{6}{18}$ b) $\frac{9}{36}$ c) $\frac{4}{12}$

14. a) $\frac{24}{30}$ b) $\frac{20}{32}$ c) $\frac{10}{16}$

15. a) $\frac{15}{36}$ b) $\frac{6}{16}$ c) $\frac{18}{48}$

16. a) $\frac{14}{16}$ b) $\frac{40}{48}$ c) $\frac{21}{24}$

17. a) $\frac{20}{36}$ b) $\frac{28}{48}$ c) $\frac{30}{54}$

18. a) $\frac{21}{27}$ b) $\frac{25}{30}$ c) $\frac{20}{24}$

19. a) $\frac{16}{48}$ b) $\frac{5}{15}$ c) $\frac{8}{18}$

20. a) $\frac{33}{36}$ b) $\frac{42}{48}$ c) $\frac{55}{60}$

21. a) $\frac{16}{18}$ b) $\frac{25}{30}$ c) $\frac{32}{36}$

22. a) $\frac{6}{40}$ b) $\frac{4}{48}$ c) $\frac{5}{60}$

23. a) $\frac{8}{60}$ b) $\frac{12}{80}$ c) $\frac{15}{100}$

24. a) $\frac{27}{60}$ b) $\frac{21}{48}$ c) $\frac{35}{80}$

25. a) $\frac{21}{36}$ b) $\frac{27}{48}$ c) $\frac{18}{32}$

Example 4

Copy the diagrams and shade in $\frac{2}{3}$ of the pattern
on each.

a)    b)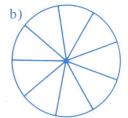

a) There are 6 equal parts, so 4 parts have to
be shaded because $\frac{4}{6} = \frac{2}{3}$.

b) There are 9 equal parts, so 6 parts have to
be shaded because $\frac{6}{9} = \frac{2}{3}$.

Exercise 30

1. Copy the diagrams and shade in $\frac{1}{2}$ of the pattern
on each.

a)   b)   c)

2. Copy the diagrams and shade in $\frac{3}{4}$ of the pattern
on each.

a)   b)   c)

3. Copy the diagrams and shade in $\frac{2}{3}$ of the pattern
on each.

a)   b)   c)

4. Copy the diagrams and shade $\frac{1}{2}$ of the pattern on each.

a) b) c)

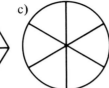

5. Copy the diagrams and shade $\frac{1}{5}$ of the pattern on each.

a) b)

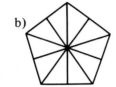

6. Copy the diagrams and shade $\frac{1}{3}$ of the pattern on each.

a) b)

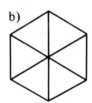

7. Copy the diagrams and shade in $\frac{1}{4}$ of the pattern on each.

a) b)

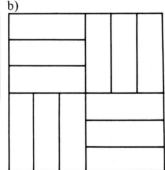

8. Copy the diagrams and shade in $\frac{1}{6}$ of the pattern on each.

a) b)

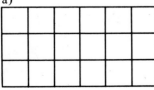

9. Copy the diagrams and shade in $\frac{2}{3}$ of the pattern on each.

a) b) c)

10. Copy the diagram and shade in $\frac{3}{4}$ of the pattern on each.

a) b)

11. Copy the diagrams and shade in $\frac{3}{5}$ of the pattern on each.

a) b)

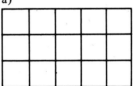

12. Copy the diagram and shade in $\frac{1}{6}$ of the pattern in blue and $\frac{1}{2}$ in red.

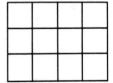

13. Copy the diagram and shade in $\frac{5}{8}$ of the pattern in blue and $\frac{1}{4}$ in red.

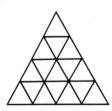

14. Copy the diagram and shade in $\frac{3}{8}$ of the pattern in red, $\frac{1}{6}$ in green, $\frac{1}{3}$ in blue and $\frac{1}{8}$ in yellow.

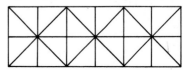

Example 5

Copy and complete by filling in the empty spaces.

a) $\frac{7}{8} = \frac{}{40}$

b) $\frac{21}{35} = \frac{3}{}$

a) $\frac{7}{8} = \frac{7 \times}{8 \times 5} = \frac{}{40}$

b) $\frac{21}{35} = \frac{21 \div 7}{35 \div} = \frac{3}{}$

$\frac{7}{8} = \frac{7 \times 5}{8 \times 5} = \frac{35}{40}$

$\frac{21}{35} = \frac{21 \div 7}{35 \div 7} = \frac{3}{5}$

$or \ \frac{7}{8} = \frac{35}{40}$ (×5)

$or \ \frac{21}{35} = \frac{3}{5}$ (÷7)

Exercise 31

Copy and complete by filling in the empty spaces.

1. $\frac{1}{3} = \frac{}{6}$ 2. $\frac{3}{4} = \frac{}{8}$ 3. $\frac{1}{2} = \frac{}{8}$ 4. $\frac{2}{5} = \frac{}{15}$

5. $\frac{1}{5} = \frac{}{20}$ 6. $\frac{3}{8} = \frac{}{32}$ 7. $\frac{1}{6} = \frac{}{30}$ 8. $\frac{5}{8} = \frac{}{40}$

9. $\frac{3}{5} = \frac{}{30}$ 10. $\frac{2}{3} = \frac{}{18}$ 11. $\frac{1}{4} = \frac{}{36}$ 12. $\frac{1}{5} = \frac{}{60}$

13. $\frac{1}{8} = \frac{2}{}$ 14. $\frac{7}{10} = \frac{14}{}$ 15. $\frac{1}{12} = \frac{3}{}$ 16. $\frac{4}{5} = \frac{12}{}$

17. $\frac{1}{9} = \frac{4}{}$ 18. $\frac{5}{7} = \frac{20}{}$ 19. $\frac{3}{8} = \frac{15}{}$ 20. $\frac{5}{6} = \frac{25}{}$

21 $\frac{4}{6} = \frac{}{3}$ 22. $\frac{10}{12} = \frac{}{6}$ 23. $\frac{9}{15} = \frac{}{5}$ 24. $\frac{21}{36} = \frac{}{12}$

25. $\frac{5}{40} = \frac{}{8}$ 26. $\frac{24}{30} = \frac{}{5}$ 27. $\frac{6}{24} = \frac{}{4}$ 28. $\frac{7}{} = \frac{35}{100}$

The top number in a fraction is called the *numerator*; the bottom number is called the *denominator*.

A *proper fraction* is a fraction in which the numerator is smaller than the denominator.

e.g. $\frac{3}{5}, \frac{4}{9}, \frac{15}{16}$

A *mixed number* is made up of a whole number and a proper fraction.

e.g. $1\frac{1}{2}, 2\frac{2}{3}, 3\frac{9}{10}$

An *improper fraction* is 'top-heavy': the numerator is greater than the denominator.

e.g. $\frac{4}{3}, \frac{23}{6}, \frac{18}{9}$

An improper fraction can be turned into a *mixed number*.

Example 6

Write $\frac{22}{6}$ as a mixed number:

$\frac{22}{6} = \frac{6}{6} + \frac{6}{6} + \frac{6}{6} + \frac{4}{6}$

$= 1 + 1 + 1 + \frac{4}{6}$

$= 3\frac{4}{6} = 3\frac{2}{3}$

Exercise 32

Write as a mixed number:

1. $\frac{7}{6}$ 2. $\frac{9}{8}$ 3. $\frac{5}{3}$ 4. $\frac{10}{7}$ 5. $\frac{11}{6}$

6. $\frac{9}{5}$ 7. $\frac{13}{8}$ 8. $\frac{17}{10}$ 9. $\frac{14}{11}$ 10. $\frac{17}{12}$

11. $\frac{10}{8}$ 12. $\frac{10}{6}$ 13. $\frac{16}{10}$ 14. $\frac{8}{6}$ 15. $\frac{15}{12}$

16. $\frac{15}{9}$ 17. $\frac{24}{15}$ 18. $\frac{12}{8}$ 19. $\frac{20}{12}$ 20. $\frac{25}{15}$

21. $\frac{5}{2}$ 22. $\frac{14}{7}$ 23. $\frac{8}{3}$ 24. $\frac{14}{5}$ 25. $\frac{18}{8}$

Example 7

Write $4\frac{7}{8}$ as an improper fraction:

$4\frac{7}{8} = 4 + \frac{7}{8}$

$= 1 + 1 + 1 + 1 + \frac{7}{8}$

$= \frac{8}{8} + \frac{8}{8} + \frac{8}{8} + \frac{8}{8} + \frac{7}{8}$

$= \frac{39}{8}$

To write a whole number as an improper fraction, put the number over a denominator of 1.

Exercise 33

Write as an improper fraction:

1. $1\frac{1}{4}$ 2. $1\frac{1}{9}$ 3. $1\frac{2}{5}$ 4. $1\frac{3}{8}$ 5. $1\frac{5}{7}$

6. $1\frac{3}{10}$ 7. $1\frac{7}{12}$ 8. $1\frac{7}{8}$ 9. $2\frac{1}{3}$ 10. $2\frac{1}{5}$

11. $2\frac{3}{4}$ 12. $2\frac{3}{5}$ 13. $2\frac{2}{7}$ 14. $3\frac{1}{2}$ 15. $3\frac{1}{5}$

16. $3\frac{2}{3}$ 17. $4\frac{1}{4}$ 18. $4\frac{3}{5}$ 19. $5\frac{1}{3}$ 20. $5\frac{2}{5}$

21. $5\frac{4}{5}$ 22. $5\frac{3}{4}$ 23. $6\frac{1}{2}$ 24. 40   25. 1

Investigation 2

Coloured patterns

Areas on a map have to be coloured differently so that the boundary between each area is clear. What is the least number of colours to be used on maps or diagrams?

For example,

a)

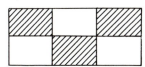

two colours needed

b)

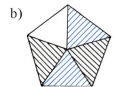

three colours needed

Copy the diagrams below and then colour them. What is the least number of colours required for each diagram if two areas having a common boundary must have a different colour?

1.

2.

3.

4.

5.

6.

7. a) Can you draw a diagram that requires more than four colours in order to avoid areas with a common side having the same colour?

   b) If the number of parts of your diagram is a multiple of the number of colours required, are all colours always used the same number of times?

8. a) Make a simple map of your area. Then colour the map so that the least number of colours are used and adjacent districts are a different colour.

   b) Choose a map showing the different states of the U.S.A. or the different countries of Africa. Copy your map and colour it with the least number of colours so that the borders are distinct.

2.2 The decimal point

1 unit

10 tenths

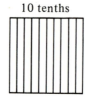

100 hundredths

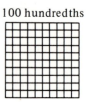

1 unit

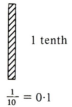

1 tenth

$\frac{1}{10} = 0{\cdot}1$

1 hundredth

$\frac{1}{100} = 0{\cdot}01$

Example 1

Write the following as a decimal

a)

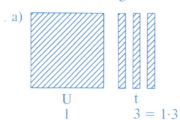

U
1

t
$3 = 1{\cdot}3$

b)

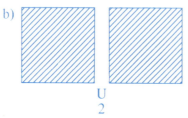 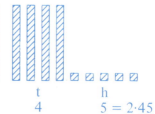

U
2

t
4

h
$5 = 2{\cdot}45$

Exercise 34

Write the following as a decimal

1.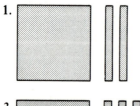

2.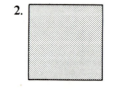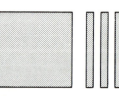

3.

4.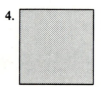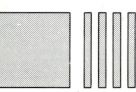

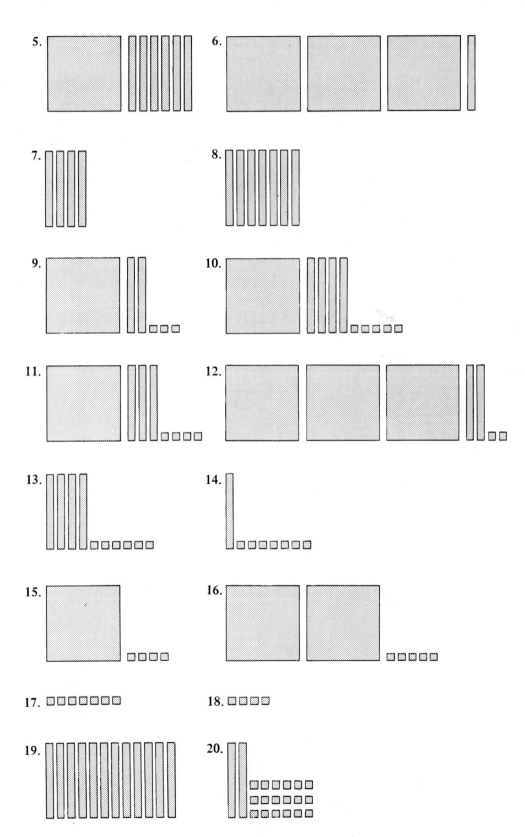

Write the shaded part as a decimal.

21. 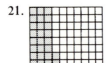   22. 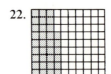   23. 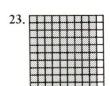   24.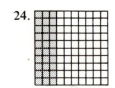

25.    26. 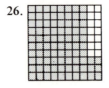   27. 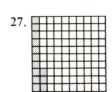   28.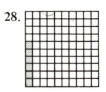

29. 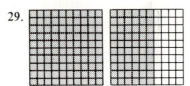   30.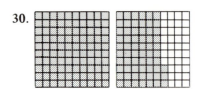

Example 2

Draw diagrams to show (a) 3·5 (b) 0·25

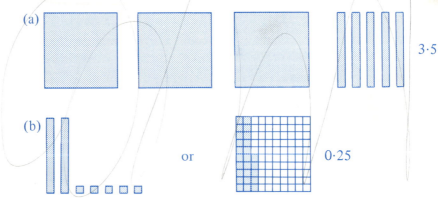

Exercise 35

Draw diagrams on squared paper to show these numbers.

1. 2·3	**2.** 1·6	**3.** 2·1	**4.** 3·2
5. 1·7	**6.** 2·4	**7.** 0·8	**8.** 0·2
9. 2·14	**10.** 1·62	**11.** 2·43	**12.** 1.72
13. 0·42	**14.** 0.35	**15.** 0·61	**16.** 1·07
17. 2.02	**18.** 0·03	**19.** 0·08	**20.** 2.50

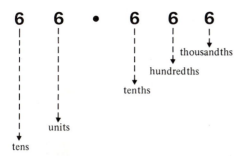

The number shown is made up of 6 tens, 6 units, 6 tenths, 6 hundredths, and 6 thousandths.

The number is read as 'sixty-six point six six six.

Note the decimal point which separates whole numbers from fractions.

Once again, the value of each digit depends upon its place value.

Example 3

Give the value of each underlined figure.

a) 4·3<u>2</u>   b) 10·4<u>7</u>   c) 1·02<u>4</u>

a) Three-tenths or $\frac{3}{10}$ or 0·3

b) Seven-hundredths or $\frac{7}{100}$ or 0·07

c) Four-thousandths or $\frac{4}{1000}$ or 0·004

Exercise 36

Give the value of each underlined figure.

1. 3·5<u>4</u>	2. 8·<u>2</u>3	3. 5·3<u>7</u>	4. <u>2</u>·19
5. 10·5<u>2</u>	6. 4·0<u>5</u>	7. 7·0<u>6</u>	8. <u>5</u>·4
9. 6·<u>1</u>	10. 3·65<u>2</u>	11. 5·84<u>7</u>	12. 1·2<u>3</u>3
13. 5·2<u>5</u>2	14. 4·6<u>7</u>1	15. 7·31<u>5</u>	16. 2·5<u>3</u>6
17. 1·84<u>5</u>	18. 6·3<u>2</u>2	19. 5·0<u>3</u>5	20. 8·04<u>4</u>
21. 9·0<u>5</u>6	22. 4·0<u>1</u>7	23. 5·30<u>4</u>	24. 2·0<u>0</u>6
25. 7·00<u>3</u>	26. 7·04<u>2</u>	27. 6·9<u>0</u>5	28. 0·5<u>4</u>1
29. 2·0<u>4</u>1	30. 0·4<u>1</u>2	31. 0·0<u>0</u>4	32. <u>5</u>·516
33. 3·1<u>4</u>5	34. 0·0<u>2</u>2	35. 17·<u>4</u>2	36. 2<u>6</u>·51
37. 34·8<u>3</u>	38. 7<u>6</u>·04	39. 0·0<u>6</u>2	40. 0·21<u>0</u>

Example 4

Arrange the following numbers in order of size, starting with the smallest.

a) 4·04, 40·4, 0·404, 404

The order is: 0·404, 4·04, 40·4, 404

b) 6, 6·006, 6·6, 6·016, 6·06

The order is: 6, 6·006, 6·016, 6·06, 6·6

The numbers in column order are:

a)   0·404   b) 6
           4·04   6·006
           40·4   6·016
           404   6·06
                             6·6

Exercise 37

Arrange the numbers in each question in order of size, starting with the smallest.

1. 5·2, 5·8, 5·0   6. 0·7, 0·9, 0·8, 0·6
2. 3·7, 2·8, 1·9   7. 1·8, 0·8, 8, 8·1
3. 2·6, 6·2, 4·4   8. 2·8, 8·31, 7·6
4. 3·6, 5, 4·1   9. 7·7, 6·83, 9
5. 1·2, 0·6, 2   10. 0·08, 0·16, 0·12

11. 2·02, 2·2, 2·12, 2·21
12. 54, 5·49, 5·5, 5·94
13. 6·6, 7·67, 6·76, 7·66
14. 5·02, 5·22, 5, 5·2
15. 4·33, 4, 4·03, 4·3
16. 7·04, 7·4, 7·004, 7·44, 7·044, 7
17. 8·005, 8·55, 8·5, 8·055, 8, 8·05
18. 3·11, 3, 3·1, 3·01, 3·011, 3·001
19. 5·03, 5·33, 0·53, 5·3
20. 7·2, 7·22, 7·02, 0·72

21. 6·05, 0·65, 6·55, 6·5
22. 3·024, 0·324, 3·24, 32·4, 3·204
23. 5·061, 56·1, 5·601, 0·561, 5·61
24. 4·803, 0·483, 4·083, 4·83, 48·3, 48·03
25. 2·705, 27·5, 2·75, 0·275, 2·075, 27·05
26. 0·243, 0·089, 0·301, 0·045, 0·405, 0·423
27. 0·2, 0·202, 0·22, 0·022, 0·222
28. 0·808, 0·88, 0·008, 0·088, 0·08
29. 40·04, 4·04, 4·404, 44·04, 4·044
30. 83·383, 83·833, 8·833, 8·3833, 83·338

Arrange the numbers in each question in order of size, starting with the largest
31. 7·2, 7·72, 72·7, 7·22
32. 0·065, 0·506, 0·65, 0·605
33. 0·023, 0·032, 0·003, 0·203
34. 7·57, 7·75, 57, 5·77
35. 10·02, 10·2, 1·202, 1·22
36. 1·13, 1·301, 1·031, 1·013, 1·31
37. 74·47, 7·474, 7·744, 47·74, 7·747
38. 0·04, 0·004, 0·404, 0·044, 0·045
39. 88·89, 89·98, 89·89, 88·99, 98·89
40. 0·2131, 0·02131, 0·01231, 0·3231, 0·03121

Example 5

Give the smallest number and the largest number that can be made using *all* the following digits and a decimal point.

a) 3, 7, 4, 1   b) 4, 0, 7   c) 2, 0, 0, 2

a) The smallest number is 1·347, the largest number is 743·1.

b) The smallest number is 0·47, the largest number is 74·0.

c) The smallest number is 0·022, the largest number is 220·0.

Note A whole number is written 740, or 740·0; never write 740· for this number. A decimal fraction is written 0·47 but never ·47.

Exercise 38

For each question give the smallest number and the largest number that can be made using *all* the digits and a decimal point.

1. 3, 5, 6	**2.** 4, 1, 8	**3.** 9, 2, 3
4. 7, 5, 4	**5.** 2, 0, 5	**6.** 6, 0, 7
7. 2, 5, 3, 1	**8.** 4, 6, 5, 7	**9.** 8, 9, 4, 3
10. 3, 6, 1, 5	**11.** 7, 2, 8, 4	**12.** 3, 0, 5, 2
13. 1, 0, 7, 8	**14.** 3, 0, 0, 4	**15.** 7, 0, 0, 9
16. 1, 1, 2, 2	**17.** 5, 5, 5, 6	**18.** 3, 2, 3, 2
19. 7, 0, 0, 7	**20.** 1, 0, 0, 0, 1	

To multiply a number by 10, you should promote each digit one place.

H T U · t h

4 · 8 1   X 10

4 8 · 1

4·81 X 10 = 48·1

To multiply a number by 100, you should promote each digit two places.

H T U · t h

3 · 6   X 100

3 6 0 ·

3·6 X 100 = 360

Example 6

a) 4·6 X 10   b) 1·1 X 100   c) 0·23 X 10
d) 0·05 X 10   e) 0·004 X 100

a) 4 · 6 X 10 = 4 6 · 0
   U · t   T U · t

b) 1 · 1 X 100 = 1 1 0
   U · t   H T U · t

c) 0·23 X 10 = 2·3

d) 0·05 X 10 = 0·5

e) 0·04 X 100 = 4

Exercise 39

Multiply each of the following by 10.

1. 3·25	**2.** 5·36	**3.** 1·84	**4.** 4·05
5. 2·08	**6.** 5·4	**7.** 8·2	**8.** 9·1
9. 0·26	**10.** 0·57	**11.** 0·89	**12.** 0·3
13. 0·9	**14.** 0·1	**15.** 0·03	**16.** 0·07
17. 0·425	**18.** 0·641	**19.** 0·118	**20.** 0·402
21. 0·105	**22.** 0·004	**23.** 0·009	**24.** 0·054
25. 0·017			

Multiply each of the following by 100.

26. 0·453	**27.** 0·627	**28.** 0·121	**29.** 0·508
30. 0·906	**31.** 0·064	**32.** 0·038	**33.** 0·005
34. 0·002	**35.** 0·36	**36.** 0·92	**37.** 0·55
38. 0·04	**39.** 0·09	**40.** 0·3	**41.** 0·8
42. 0·1	**43.** 5·27	**44.** 3·94	**45.** 1·22
46. 2·03	**47.** 6·06	**48.** 5·2	**49.** 3·9
50. 1·1			

To divide a number by 10, you should demote each digit one place.

H   T   U · t   h

4   1 · 7   ÷ 10

4 · 1   7

$41.7 \div 10 = 4.17$

To divide a number by 100, you should demote each digit two places.

H   T   U · t   h

2   4   3   ÷ 100

2 · 4   3

$243 \div 100 = 2.43$

Example 7

Work out the following.

a) $6.4 \div 10$ b) $6 \div 10$ c) $7.3 \div 100$
d) $0.4 \div 100$

a) 6 · 4 ÷ 10 = 0 · 64
   U · t   U · t h

b) 6   ÷ 10 = 0 · 6
   U   U · t

c) 7·3   ÷ 100 = 0·073

d) 0·4   ÷ 100 = 0·004

Exercise 40

Divide each of the following by 10.

1. 5·6	**2.** 3·2	**3.** 9·7	**4.** 4·35
5. 1·58	**6.** 2·16	**7.** 3·09	**8.** 5
9. 8	**10.** 2	**11.** 25·4	**12.** 67·1
13. 95·7	**14.** 50·6	**15.** 32	**16.** 75
17. 99	**18.** 0·19	**19.** 0·83	**20.** 0·55
21. 0·3	**22.** 0·7	**23.** 0·1	**24.** 0·05
25. 0·02			

Divide each of the following by 100.

26. 35·2	**27.** 81·6	**28.** 40·5	**29.** 20·1
30. 37	**31.** 62	**32.** 50	**33.** 125
34. 236	**35.** 5·34	**36.** 9·95	**37.** 4·74
38. 1·08	**39.** 5·8	**40.** 3·6	**41.** 1·5
42. 0·27	**43.** 0·61	**44.** 0·32	**45.** 0·05
46. 0·08	**47.** 0·04	**48.** 0·8	**49.** 0·3
50. 0·1			

2.3   Addition and subtraction of decimals

To add decimal fractions, the decimal points are put underneath each other to make sure that each figure is in its proper place.

Example 1

Add to find the 'odd answer out'.

a) 0·4 + 0·5 + 0·6   b) 0·2 + 0·7 + 0·6
c) 0·9 + 0·7 + 0·9   d) 0·8 + 0·2 + 0·5

a)   0·4   b)   0·2   c)   0·9   d)   0·8
      0·5   0·7   0·7   0·2
    + 0·6   + 0·6   + 0·9   + 0·5
    ─────   ─────   ─────   ─────
      1·5   1·5   2·5   1·5
    ─────   ─────   ─────   ─────

So c) is the 'odd answer out'.

Example 2

Add to find the 'odd answer out'

a) 3·46 + 1·2 + 5·36   (hint: write 1·2 as 1·20)
b) 3·34 + 4   + 2·78   (hint: write 4 as 4·00)
c) 2·14 + 5·08 + 2·9   (hint: write 2·9 as 2·90)

a)   3·46   b)   3·34   c)   2·14
      1·20   4·00   5·08
    + 5·36   + 2·78   + 2·90
    ─────   ─────   ─────
     10·02   10·12   10·12
    ─────   ─────   ─────

So a) is the 'odd answer out'.

Exercise 41

Add to find the 'odd answer out'.

1. a) 0·2 + 0·7 + 0·4   2. a) 0·6 + 0·8 + 0·4
   b) 0·6 + 0·1 + 0·8   b) 0·5 + 0·9 + 0·2
   c) 0·3 + 0·2 + 0·8   c) 0·4 + 0·5 + 0·7
   d) 0·7 + 0·3 + 0·3   d) 0·3 + 0·8 + 0·5

3. a) 0·9 + 0·8 + 0·6   4. a) 0·9 + 0·7 + 0·8
   b) 0·6 + 0·5 + 1·2   b) 0·2 + 0·5 + 1·5
   c) 1·2 + 0·7 + 0·4   c) 1·3 + 0·4 + 0·7
   d) 0·6 + 0·8 + 0·7   d) 1·1 + 1·2 + 0·1

5. a) 1·3 + 0·5 + 0·8   6. a) 1·4 + 1·5 + 0·3
   b) 0·4 + 1·7 + 0·5   b) 0·2 + 1·7 + 1·5
   c) 1·2 + 1·4 + 0·2   c) 1·7 + 0·9 + 0·6
   d) 0·9 + 0·9 + 0·8   d) 0·5 + 1·8 + 0·9

7. a) 1·5 + 1·3 + 1·8   8. a) 2·8 + 1·9 + 0·8
   b) 2·8 + 0·6 + 1·4   b) 2·5 + 2·8 + 0·4
   c) 3·8 + 0·7 + 0·3   c) 1·5 + 0·9 + 3·3
   d) 2·2 + 2·5 + 0·1   d) 2·2 + 1·4 + 2·1

9. a) 2·5 + 2·3 + 1·6   10. a) 5·8 + 1·4 + 1·9
   b) 3·2 + 1·5 + 1·7   b) 2·7 + 3·8 + 2·6
   c) 1·8 + 0·7 + 3·9   c) 4·2 + 3·5 + 1·6
   d) 2·8 + 0·9 + 2·9   d) 5·1 + 3·4 + 0·6

Excercise 42

Add to find the 'odd answer out'.

1. a) 2·13 + 4·37 + 3·12   2. a) 2·63 + 1·4 + 2·5
   b) 2·65 + 4·21 + 2·56   b) 2·1 + 3·38 + 1·15
   c) 5·81 + 2·37 + 1·44   c) 2·89 + 0·24 + 3·5

3. a) 5·49 + 2·8 + 2·46   4. a) 8·43 + 4·07 + 2·82
   b) 4·93 + 3·09 + 2·75   b) 5·78 + 3·44 + 6·2
   c) 5·97 + 1·78 + 3   c) 2·09 + 4·33 + 9

5. a) 5·65 + 0·81 + 2·44   6. a) 6·5 + 9·84 + 3·66
   b) 4·73 + 1·02 + 2·34   b) 9·57 + 4·43 + 7
   c) 2·53 + 5·2 + 1·17   c) 8·91 + 5·03 + 6·06

7. a) 11·24 + 10·31 + 13·45
   b) 11·52 + 12·36 + 12·12
   c) 13·2 + 12·67 + 10·13

8. a) 15·24 + 12·3 + 14·46
   b) 13·12 + 11·6 + 15·28
   c) 14·87 + 13·13 + 12

9. a) 14·25 + 11·1 + 1·65
   b) 11·38 + 12 + 3·62
   c) 12·19 + 3 + 10·81

10. a) 13 + 0·74 + 6·2
    b) 10·3 + 0·04 + 9·6
    c) 8·6 + 0·24 + 3·9

To subtract decimal fractions, once again make sure that the figures are in their right places by putting the decimal points underneath each other.

Example 3

Subtract to find the 'odd answer out'.

a) $2 \cdot 6 - 1 \cdot 4$ b) $2 \cdot 4 - 1 \cdot 2$
c) $3 \cdot 7 - 2 \cdot 5$ d) $9 \cdot 6 - 8 \cdot 5$

a)	2·6	b)	2·4	c)	3·7	d)	9·6
	− 1·4		− 1·2		− 2·5		− 8·5
	1·2		1·2		1·2		1·1

So d) is the 'odd answer out'.

Example 4

Subtract to find the 'odd answer out'.

a) $4 - 2 \cdot 6$ (write 4 as 4·0)
b) $5 \cdot 2 - 2 \cdot 8$
c) $9 - 6 \cdot 6$ (write 9 as 9·0)
d) $6 \cdot 6 - 4 \cdot 2$

a)	4·0	b)	5·2	c)	9·0	d)	6·6
	− 2·6		− 2·8		− 6·6		− 4·2
	1·4		2·4		2·4		2·4

So a) is the 'odd answer out'.

Exercise 43

Subtract to find the 'odd answer out'.

1. a) $3 \cdot 9 - 2 \cdot 3$
   b) $6 \cdot 6 - 5 \cdot 2$
   c) $5 \cdot 5 - 4 \cdot 1$
   d) $2 \cdot 8 - 1 \cdot 4$

2. a) $5 \cdot 6 - 3 \cdot 4$
   b) $8 \cdot 9 - 6 \cdot 5$
   c) $9 \cdot 3 - 7 \cdot 1$
   d) $3 \cdot 5 - 1 \cdot 3$

3. a) $7 \cdot 8 - 3 \cdot 3$
   b) $5 \cdot 9 - 1 \cdot 4$
   c) $8 \cdot 7 - 4 \cdot 1$
   d) $6 \cdot 5 - 2$

4. a) $6 \cdot 9 - 1 \cdot 8$
   b) $8 \cdot 7 - 3 \cdot 5$
   c) $9 \cdot 6 - 4 \cdot 4$
   d) $7 \cdot 8 - 2 \cdot 6$

5. a) $6 \cdot 9 - 1 \cdot 4$
   b) $7 \cdot 8 - 2 \cdot 3$
   c) $9 \cdot 7 - 4 \cdot 1$
   d) $8 \cdot 5 - 3$

6. a) $4 \cdot 4 - 1 \cdot 8$
   b) $6 \cdot 5 - 3 \cdot 9$
   c) $7 \cdot 1 - 4 \cdot 5$
   d) $5 \cdot 2 - 2 \cdot 7$

7. a) $5 \cdot 2 - 2 \cdot 3$
   b) $7 \cdot 5 - 4 \cdot 6$
   c) $6 \cdot 6 - 3 \cdot 8$
   d) $8 \cdot 3 - 5 \cdot 4$

8. a) $8 \cdot 2 - 3 \cdot 4$
   b) $6 \cdot 5 - 1 \cdot 7$
   c) $7 \cdot 4 - 2 \cdot 6$
   d) $9 \cdot 7 - 4 \cdot 8$

9. a) $9 \cdot 3 - 4 \cdot 5$
   b) $6 \cdot 6 - 1 \cdot 8$
   c) $8 \cdot 4 - 3 \cdot 7$
   d) $5 \cdot 2 - 0 \cdot 4$

Example 5

Subtract to find the difference between the following pairs of numbers and so find the 'odd answer out'.

a) 7·5 and 1·26   (write 7·5 as 7·50)
b) 34 and 27·66   (write 34 as 34·00)
c) 10·63 and 4·39

a)	7·50	b)	34·00	c)	10·63
	− 1·26		− 27·66		− 4·39
	6·24		6·34		6·24

So b) is the 'odd answer out'.

Exercise 44

Subtract to find the difference between the following pairs of numbers and so find the 'odd answer out'.

1. a) 8·59 and 3·25
   b) 6·62 and 1·38
   c) 9·23 and 3·89

2. a) 8·32 and 2·87
   b) 9·04 and 3·49
   c) 7·07 and 1·52

3. a) 5·49 and 0·86
   b) 5·17 and 0·64
   c) 9·62 and 5·09

4. a) 7·27 and 2·9
   b) 4·87 and 0·4
   *c) 5·17 and 0·8

5. a) 5·2 and 1·66
   b) 8 and 4·46
   c) 6·7 and 3·06

6. a) 46·97 and 36·45
   b) 28·18 and 17·93
   c) 14·02 and 3·77

7. a) 22·63 and 7·49
   b) 38·06 and 22·92
   c) 42·91 and 28·76

8. a) 32·09 and 23·53
   b) 20·73 and 12·08
   c) 16 and 7·44

9. a) 0·4 and 1·62
   b) 0·616 and 1·736
   c) 0·58 and 1·8

10. a) 2·7 and 2·34
    b) 4·6 and 5·04
    c) 3·22 and 2·78

11. a) 6·8 and 2·08
    b) 4·81 and 0·09
    c) 4·6 and 0·08

12. a) 60·87 and 38·82
    b) 4·5 and 19·48
    c) 28·6 and 6·55

13. a) 2·3 and 3·04
    b) 1·59 and 2·33
    c) 0·45 and 1·09

14. a) 30·3 and 9·28
    b) 23·02 and 2·9
    c) 43·11 and 22·99

15. a) 1·72 and 4
    b) 3·9 and 6·18
    c) 2·17 and 4·4

16. a) 10·008 and 9·78
    b) 0·213 and 0·085
    c) 12·872 and 13

3 Time and money

3.1 The calendar

The days of the week are:

Sunday, Monday, Tuesday, Wednesday, Thursday, Friday, Saturday.

The months of the year are:

1. January with 31 days
2. February with 28 or 29 days
3. March with 31 days
4. April with 30 days
5. May with 31 days
6. June with 30 days
7. July with 31 days
8. August with 31 days
9. September with 30 days
10. October with 31 days
11. November with 30 days
12. December with 31 days.

Here is a rhyme to help you to remember.

Thirty days in September,
*   April, June and November,*
All the rest have thirty-one
*   Except February alone,*
Which has twenty-eight days clear
*   And twenty-nine each leap year.*

A leap year occurs every four years; 1980 was a leap year, and 1984, 1988, 1992 and 1996 are all leap years.

Exercise 45

Write down the day of the week which is:

1. the day before Thursday
2. the day before Sunday
3. the day after Monday
4. the day after Saturday
5. two days before Tuesday
6. three days after Wednesday
7. four days before Monday
8. five days after Friday
9. six days before Thursday
10. seven days after Wednesday.

Write down the month of the year which is:

11. the third month
12. the seventh month
13. the tenth month
14. the month after July
15. the month before October
16. two months after March
17. four months before February
18. six months after January
19. nine months after October
20. eleven months after April.

21. On Tuesday Millicent said her birthday would be in three days. Which day was her birthday?
22. On Monday the teacher told the class they had to hand in their homework exercise two days later. On which day was the exercise to be handed in?
23. The cup tie on Saturday ended in a draw.

The replay was three days later. On which day was the replay?

24. Patrick planted some seeds and put them on the window sill to grow. On Sunday, six days after Patrick planted them, the first green shoots appeared. On which day did Patrick plant the seeds?
25. Dave took his watch to the shop on Saturday for repair. The shop told him it would be ready in ten days. On which day of the week will the watch be ready for collection?
26. The snow came in December and stayed for three months. In which month did the snow finally disappear?

27. In October Samantha was selected for the school chess team, only three months after her twelfth birthday. In which month was her birthday?
28. Look at the newspaper below.

In which month did the shop open?

Example 1

a) Write the 13th of March 1979 in number form.
b) Write 11/10/68 in words.

a) 13/3/79
b) The eleventh of October, nineteen hundred and sixty-eight.

Exercise 46

Write these dates in number form.
1. 10th March 1969
2. 11th July 1974
3. 21st September 1981
4. 17th November 1986
5. 31st October 1961
6. 10th January 1954
7. 17th June 1995
8. The tenth day of May, nineteen hundred and fifty-six.
9. The twenty-fifth day of August, nineteen hundred and seventy-seven.
10. The fifteenth day of November, nineteen hundred and eighty-four.

Write these dates in words.
11. 2/3/74
12. 13/10/62
13. 16/5/85
14. 17/9/80
15. 26/7/73
16. 30-1-55
17. 29:2:84
18. 5-4-77
19. 150662
20. 31/9/55 What is wrong with this date?

Another way of remembering the number of days in each month is to use your knuckles as follows.

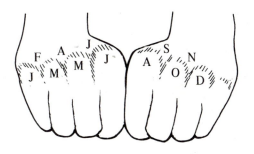

The months on top of the knuckles have 31 days. The months in between the knuckles have 30 days except February.

January					February				
S		7	14	21	28		4	11	18	25
M	1	8	15	22	29		5	12	19	26
T	2	9	16	23	30		6	13	20	27
W	3	10	17	24	31		7	14	21	28
T	4	11	18	25		1	8	15	22
F	5	12	19	26		2	9	16	23
S	6	13	20	27		3	10	17	24

Example 2

a) How many days from January 15th to February 12th?

Days left in January $= 31 - 15 = 16$
Days in February $\quad = 12$

Therefore, the number of days
$= 16 + 12 = 28$

b) What date is 14 days before February 5th?

Days in February $= 5$
Days in January $= 14 - 5 = 9$

Therefore, date in January $= 31 - 9 = 22$nd

Exercise 47

How many days from:
1. January 21st to January 26th
2. February 8th to February 22nd
3. May 10th to May 29th
4. November 1st to November 26th
5. September 18th to September 30th
6. January 19th to February 15th
7. January 11th to February 26th
8. January 2nd to February 7th
9. January 9th to February 6th
10. March 8th to April 14th
11. January 25th to February 3rd
12. January 20th to February 17th
13. May 22nd to June 24th
14. January 30th to February 13th
15. January 31st to February 27th?

What is the date:
16. 10 days before 24th January
17. 7 days before 11th February
18. 22 days before 28th February
19. 17 days after 13th January
20. 12 days after 8th February
21. 6 days before February 4th
22. 15 days before February 11th
23. 19 days before April 9th
24. 16 days before February 2nd
25. 23 days before June 8th
26. 8 days after January 26th
27. 12 days after January 23rd
28. 15 days after March 18th
29. 25 days after January 11th
30. 33 days after January 7th?

How many days from:
31. 27th February to 10th March, 1985
32. 3rd February to 25th March, 1988
33. 26th February to 12th March, 1990
34. 22nd February to 30th March, 1992
35. 12th February to 2nd March, 1994?

What is the date
36. 26 days before March 21st, 1986
37. 34 days after February 23rd, 1988
38. 49 days after January 21st, 1991
39. 35 days before March 10th, 1992
40. 28 days before March 1st, 1996?

Example 3

How many days from March 20th to June 24th?

Days in March $= 31 - 20 = 11$
Days in April, May $= 30 + 31 = 61$
Days in June $= 24$

Therefore, the number of days $=$
$11 + 61 + 24 = 96$

Exercise 48

How many days from:
1. March 25th to June 8th
2. May 22nd to August 14th
3. October 26th to January 21st
4. July 18th to October 5th
5. April 15th to July 16th
6. September 17th to December 23rd
7. June 8th to September 4th
8. November 6th to February 15th
9. March 27th to July 3rd
10. August 23rd to December 10th?

11. May 28th to September 25th
12. October 14th to February 6th
13. July 11th to November 18th
14. April 12th to August 24th
15. September 5th to January 6th
16. June 3rd to October 10th
17. May 9th to July 28th
18. October 13th to December 7th
19. July 19th to September 11th
20. April 16th to June 20th?

21. Pia bought a big tube of toothpaste on 27th March and used it twice a day until 10th June. How many days did the toothpaste last?
22. The summer holidays started on 12th July and finished on 1st September. How long did they last?
23. Jane's birthday was on the 17th April and Mary's birthday was on the 25th January. How many days earlier was Mary's birthday in 1985?

24. A long distance walker left John o' Groats on 7th July and arrived at Lands End on 10th August. How long did his journey take?

25. Mr Ashad ordered a new Jaguar car on 11th November 1984 but he did not receive it until 5th March 1985. How many days did he have to wait?

26. Workmen started laying a section of gas pipeline on 17th April and finished on 26th October. How long did it take them?

27. A lone sailor left New York on 10th June and landed in Plymouth on 8th September. How many days did he take to cross the Atlantic Ocean?

28. Janet planted a row of potatoes on 10th April and lifted them on 17th July. How many days were there between planting and lifting the potatoes?

29. A round-the-world cruise left Southampton on 25th October 1983 and returned on 16th March 1984. How long did the cruise last?

30. If the shop conversion started on 28th September, how many days have the workmen got to complete the conversion?

Fashion Fare Opens 10th November

Example 4

a) John's father was born in 1948. How many years old is he in 1987?

$(1987 - 1948) = 39$. He is 39 years old.

b) John is aged 12 in 1987. In what year was he born?

$(1987 - 12) = 1975$. He was born in 1975.

Exercise 49

Find how many years old each of the following persons is in 1988. Their year of birth is given.

1. 1980	**2.** 1976	**3.** 1972	**4.** 1966
5. 1961	**6.** 1955	**7.** 1951	**8.** 1944
9. 1937	**10.** 1932	**11.** 1925	**12.** 1917
13. 1908	**14.** 1904	**15.** 1892	

When were each of the following members of a family born? Their age in 1987 is given.

16. Tom, 3 years.
17. Mary, 7 years.
18. Julie, 9 years.
19. Peter, 13 years.
20. Aunt Pam, 24 years.
21. Uncle Bert, 27 years.
22. Mum, 32 years.
23. Dad, 38 years.
24. Aunt Jane, 45 years.
25. Uncle Fred, 49 years.
26. Grannie, 63 years.
27. Grandad, 66 years.
28. Great-Uncle Robert, 75 years.
29. Great-Grannie, 87 years.
30. Great-Grandad, 91 years.

Example 5

The first bicycle was invented in 1801. How many years was this before 1987?

In 1987, this was $1987 - 1801 = 186$ years ago.

Exercise 50

How long ago did these events take place?
1. The Battle of Hastings, 1066.
2. The Battle of Waterloo, 1815.
3. The Great Fire of London, 1666.
4. The Spanish Armada, 1588.
5. The Battle of Bannockburn, 1314.
6. The start of the First World War, 1914.
7. The Queen's coronation, 1953.
8. Man's first landing on the Moon, 1969.
9. The Roman's leaving Britain, 410.
10. The building of Hadrian's Wall, 126.

11. The death of Alfred the Great, 899.
12. The coronation of Macbeth, 1040.
13. The death of Alexander, 1057.
14. The first motor car, 1876.
15. The death of William the Conqueror, 1087.
16. The coronation of Elizabeth I, 1558.
17. The execution of Charles I, 1649.
18. The coronation of Alfred the Great, 871.
19. The birth of Lloyd George, 1865.
20. The death of Flora MacDonald, 1790.

To find your age in years and months, you subtract your date of birth from the present date. If the day of your birth is greater than the day in the present date, subtract one month.

Example 6

Brenda's date of birth is 10/12/72 and her brother George's is 30/5/70. How old are they in years and months on 23rd October 1987?

		Year	Month
Brenda:	Present date	87^{86}	10^{22}
	Date of birth	72	12
		14 y	10 m

Brenda is 14 years 10 months old.

		Year	Month	Day
George:	Present date	87	10	(23)
	Date of birth	70	5	(30)
		17 y	5 m	
		—	1 m	
		17 y	4 m	

George is 17 years 4 months old.

Exercise 51

Find the ages in years and months of the following people on 23rd October 1988. Their dates of birth are given after their name.

1. Andrew 13/1/83   2. Brian 15/3/81
3. Claire 22/6/80   4. Dorothy 20/7/79
5. Elaine 2/9/76   6. Frank 1/2/75
7. Graeme 20/10/72   8. Helen 14/12/70
9. Ivy 21/11/66   10. Jennifer 22/12/62

11. Kevin 14/4/82   12. Linda 2/5/77
13. Michael 1/11/74   14. Norma 30/1/73
15. Oliver 28/5/71   16. Penny 27/11/69
17. Robert 14/12/59   18. Susan 30/12/55
19. Trevor 24/10/52   20. Zara 30/11/1898

21. To play in the under 15 basketball team in the season 1987-8, a player must be under 15 on the 1st September 1987. Which of the following can play in the under 15 team? Their dates of birth are given.

Alice 2/10/72
Grace 13/6/72
Mary 14/12/73
Lai Ling 22/1/72
Jameela 30/8/72
Theresa 29/9/72

Investigation 3A

The Calendar

September comes from the Latin word for 7 (Septem). October comes from the Latin word for 8 (Octo).

In early Roman times September was the seventh month of the year and October was the eighth month of the year.

1. Find out why September and October are now the ninth and tenth months of the year.
2. How did the other months of the year get their names?
3. How did the days of the weeks get their names?
4. When September was the seventh month, how many days were there in each month?
5. What names did the Romans have for the days of the week?
6. Find out about the Chinese calendar, and why its years are named after animals.

Hint: Use the school library. You may find an encyclopedia useful.

3.2   Reading the time _____

Here are three ways of representing time, on a clock face (analogue), as numbers (digital) and in words.

4:05

five past four

5:45

five forty-five
or quarter to six

Exercise 52

Write down the time as shown on the clock faces
 a) in numbers
 b) in words (two ways if possible)

1.  2.

3.  4.

5.  6.

7. 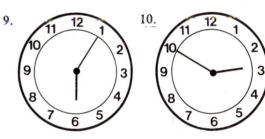 8.

9. 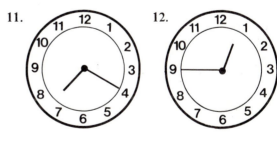 10.

11. 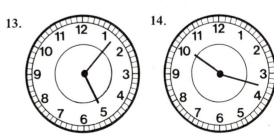 12.

13. 14.

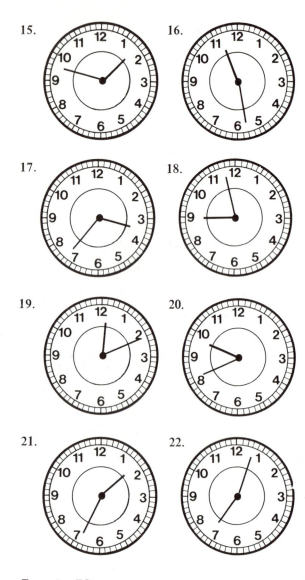

15.   16.

17.   18.

19.   20.

21.   22.

Exercise 53

Draw hands on a clock face to show the following times.

1. 3.30   2. 8.45   3. 10.20
4. 7.15   5. 4.40   6. 11.35

7. 2 o' clock   8. half past five
9. ten to four   10. twenty five past nine

11. 3.12   12. 7.29   13. 6.58
14. 6.04   15. 12.27   16. 9 42

17. quarter to eleven
18. four minutes to seven
19. twenty-two minutes past ten
20. twenty-five minutes to four

Noon is twelve o'clock midday.

am means before noon; pm means after noon

A time before noon has am after the numbers.
A time after noon has pm after the numbers.

Only 12.00 noon and 12.00 midnight do not need am or pm after the numbers.

Example 1

Write these times, using am or pm:

a) Breakfast is at eight o'clock in the morning.

b) Denise came home from the disco at ten past ten at night.

a) Breakfast is at 8 am
b) Denise came home at 10.10 pm

Exercise 54

Write these times, using am or pm.

1. 6.15 in the morning   2. 9.30 in the morning
3. 11.45 in the morning   4. 2.20 in the afternoon
5. 3.50 in the afternoon   6. 5.40 in the evening
7. 7.25 in the evening   8. 9.15 in the evening
9. 10.30 at night   10. 11.45 at night

11. 3.00 in the morning   12. 4.50 in the afternoon
13. midday   14. 6.20 in the morning
15. 6.45 in the evening   16. 11.15 at night
17. 12.30 lunchtime   18. 12.15 at night
19. midnight   20. 2 minutes past midnight

21. School starts at nine o'clock in the morning.
22. Tom went to the coffee morning at half past ten.
23. The football match started at 3 o'clock in the afternoon.
24. Gita went to the disco at half past seven in the evening.
25. John and Andrew sat down at five past five to watch 'Blue Peter'.
26. Sandra got off the bus at half past midnight.
27. Mum starts work at the factory at seven thirty in the morning.
28. The pupils got a half day and went home at 12 o'clock.
29. The police were called to quell the disturbance at twenty to two in the morning.
30. The street lights were switched on at quarter to eight in the evening.

3.3 Adding and subtracting time

Example 1

Write down these times.

 a) 25 minutes after 1.15 pm.

 b) 40 minutes before 8.20 am.

a)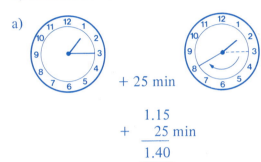

+ 25 min

$$1.15$$
$$+ \quad 25 \text{ min}$$
$$\overline{1.40}$$

25 minutes after 1.15 pm is 1.40 pm.

b)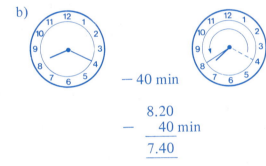

− 40 min

$$8.20$$
$$- \quad 40 \text{ min}$$
$$\overline{7.40}$$

40 minutes before 8.20 am is 7.40 am.

Exercise 55

Write down these times.

 1. 30 minutes after 5.30 pm.
 2. 15 minutes after 2.15 pm.
 3. 20 minutes after 6.50 am.
 4. 40 minutes after 10.30 am.
 5. 10 minutes after 2.55 pm.
 6. 30 minutes before noon.
 7. 20 minutes before 3.45 pm.
 8. 15 minutes before 7.10 am.
 9. 45 minutes before 10.15 pm.
10. 10 minutes before 9.00 am.

11. 2½ hours after 3.45 pm.
12. quarter of an hour before 11.00 am.
13. 12 minutes after 11.52 am.

14. 3¼ hours before noon.
15. three quarters of an hour after 4.40 pm.
16. 25 minutes before 11.09 pm.
17. 38 minutes later than 9.52 am.
18. half an hour after 3.48 pm.
19. 19 minutes earlier than 6.06 pm.
20. 35 minutes after 9.42 am.

21. The class started at 10.25 am, and John arrived 7 minutes late. At what time did John arrive?
22. The train was supposed to arrive at 6.20 pm.

STATION ANNOUNCEMENT

THE TRAIN DUE TO ARRIVE FROM GLASGOW AT 6.20 pm IS RUNNING 24 MINUTES LATE.

At what time did the train arrive?
23. The play started at 7.30 pm. To get ready, the actors had to arrive 40 minutes earlier. At what time did the actors have to arrive?
24. The film should have started at 10.50 pm, but the sports programme overran by 12 minutes. At what time did the film start?
25. The accident happened at 11.53 pm. The ambulance came 9 minutes after the accident. At what time did it arrive?
26. The second half of a football match started at 3.56 pm. The winning goal was scored 24 minutes into the second half. At what time was the goal scored?
27. The cricket match started at 11.30 am. Rain stopped play after an hour and three quarters. At what time did rain stop play?
28. The hockey match should have started at a quarter past four, but the visiting team was delayed. At what time did the match start, if the start was 27 minutes late.
29. The pop concert started at 7.30 pm. The main band was not due to appear until 1 hour 40 minutes later. At what time did the band appear?
30. Paula finished work at 5.30 pm. Her journey home took 50 minutes. At what time did she get home?

Example 2

a) The swimming lesson starts at 9.45 am and finishes at 10.35 am. How long does it last?

Lesson begins . . .   Lesson ends . . .

$$
\begin{array}{r}
9\ 95 \\
\cancel{10.35} \\
-\quad 9.45 \\
\hline
50 \text{ min.}
\end{array}
$$

The lesson lasts 50 minutes.

b) A train leaves Aberdeen at 7.50 am and arrives in Edinburgh at 10.13 am. How long does the journey take?

Journey begins . . .   Journey ends . . .

$$
\begin{array}{r}
9\ 73 \\
\cancel{10.13} \\
-\quad 7.50 \\
\hline
2h\ 23\,\text{min.}
\end{array}
$$

The journey takes 2 hours 23 minutes.

Exercise 56

How long is it from:

1. 3.30 pm to 3.50 pm   2. 4.10 pm to 4.45 pm
3. 7.05 am to 7.55 am   4. 10.45 am to 10.55 am
5. 2.30 pm to 3.00 pm   6. 6.40 am to 7.00 am
7. 10.45 am to 11.35 am   8. 9.15 pm to 10.30 pm
9. 7.05 am to 9.20 am   10. 10.25 am to 11.15 am

11. 2.53 pm to 3.07 pm   12. 8.42 am to 9.36 am
13. 12.30 pm to 1.10 pm   14. 8.20 am to 9.05 am
15. 9.53 am to 11.17 am   16. 7.25 pm to 10.05 pm
17. 5.32 pm to 8.00 pm   18. 11.25 am to 2.15 pm
19. 7.53 am to 9.16 am   20. 8.00 am to 10.30 pm?

21. Diane did not get on the 8.17 am bus because it was full. She had to wait for the next bus at 8.30 am. How much longer did she have to wait?
22. The football match started at 2.30 pm. Because of snow it was abandoned at 3.08 pm. How long did the match last?
23. An aeroplane leaves London Airport (Heathrow) at 11.05 am and arrives at Manchester Airport at 11.50 am. How long does the flight take?
24. A film show at a cinema starts at 2.30 pm and finishes at 4.45 pm. How long does it last?
25. At a school, the morning interval starts at 10.55 am and finishes at 11.15 am. How long does the interval last?
26. A ferry leaves Dover at 2.40 pm and arrives in Calais at 4.18 pm. How long does the voyage take?
27. A newspaper girl begins her delivery round at 4.20 pm and finishes at 5.35 pm. How long does it take her to complete her round?
28. Look at this poster:

ROCK CONCERT
'THE TUNELESS'

FROM: September 5–15
TICKETS: £6, £4, £2·50
BOX OFFICE OPEN: 4.45 pm to 8.15 pm

How long is the box office open for?
29. A ship leaves Liverpool at 1.15 pm and arrives at Douglas (Isle of Man) at 5.08 pm. How long does the journey take?
30. The film on BBC finished at 11.15 pm. The film on ITV started at 10.35 pm. How long were both films on at the same time?

3.4   Money — counting and writing

In the United Kingdom, we use these coins:

one p   two p   five p   ten p

twenty p   fifty p   one pound

One pound is equal to 100 pence.

$£1 = 100p$

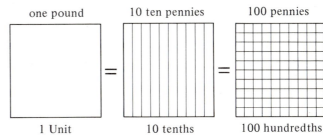

one pound   10 ten pennies   100 pennies

= =

1 Unit   10 tenths   100 hundredths

We can show one pound thirty-four like this:

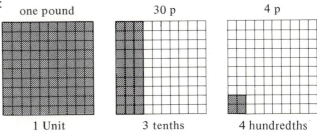

one pound   30 p   4 p

1 Unit   3 tenths   4 hundredths

We can also show one pound thirty-four like this:

U	t	h	
1	3	4	$= £1.34$

So   £1.34 means one pound thirty-four
      £0.25 means twenty-five pence.
      £1.05 means one pound and five pence.

Exercise 57

Write these sums of money as numbers.
1. one pound twenty-two pence
2. two pounds fifty-six pence
3. three pounds eighty pence
4. four pounds ninety-six pence
5. thirty-seven pence
6. fifty pence
7. four pounds and eight pence
8. twenty pounds sixty-six pence
9. two pounds six pence
10. a pound and a penny.

Write these sums of money in words.
11. £1·63
12. £2·29
13. £3·51
14. 64p
15. 19p
16. £2·90
17. £6·05
18. £1·08
19. £0·28
20. £10·20
21. 4p
22. £0·06
23. £1·60
24. £2·05
25. £0·80

For the sums of money below, choose the correct way of writing them as numbers. There may be more than one answer.
26. thirty-five pence
    a) £0·35   b) £3·50   c) 35p   d) £3·05
27. two pounds twenty pence
    a) £2·02   b) £2·2   c) £22   d) £2·20
28. ten pence
    a) £0·1   b) 10p   c) £0·10   d) 0·1p
29. one pound seven pence
    a) 1·7p   b) £1·7   c) £1·70   d) £1·07
30. three pounds sixty pence
    a) 3·60p   b) £3·06   c) £3·60   d) £3·60p

You know that 100p = £1, so to convert pounds to pence you *multiply* by 100.
To convert pence to pounds you *divide* by 100.

Example 1

Express   a) £1·32 in pence
           b) 204p in pounds and pence

a) £1·32 = (1·32 × 100)p = 132p
b) 204p = £(204 ÷ 100)   = £2·04

Exercise 58

Convert the following into pence.
1. £2·20
2. £1·62
3. £3·02
4. £10·50
5. £5·15
6. £12
7. £8
8. £20
9. £30
10. £0·34
11. £0·60
12. £0·95
13. £0·07
14. £0·02
15. £400

Convert the following into pounds and pence.
16. 154p
17. 234p
18. 385p
19. 220p
20. 460p
21. 74p
22. 30p
23. 56p
24. 8p
25. 3p
26. 7p
27. 4060p
28. 3840p
29. 7000p
30. 30 500p

Example 2

Simon had these coins in his pocket.

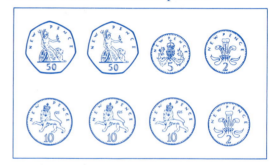

How much did he have?

Simon had:
50p + 50p + 10p + 10p + 10p + 5p + 2p + 2p
= 139p
= £1·39

Exercise 59

Work out how much money there is in each box.

1.

2.

3.
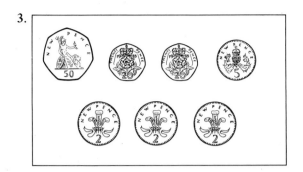

4.

5.

6.
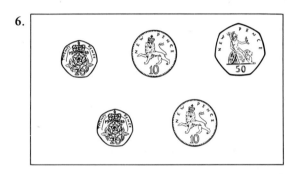

7.
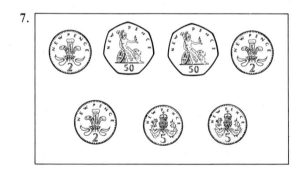

8.
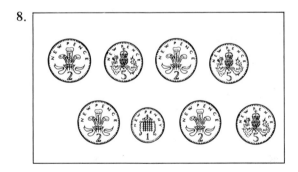

9.

10.

Example 3

A shop till has this number of coins in each compartment.

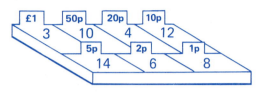

How much money is in the till?

3	£1	coins	= £	3·00
10	50p	coins	= £	5·00
4	20p	coins	= £	0·80
12	10p	coins	= £	1·20
14	5p	coins	= £	0·70
6	2p	coins	= £	0·12
8	1p	coins	= £	0·08
		total	=	£10·90

There is £10·90 in the till.

Exercise 60

Find how much money there is in each till.

1.

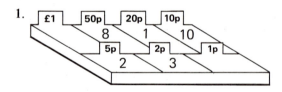

2.

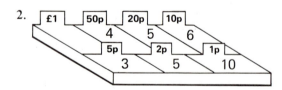

3.

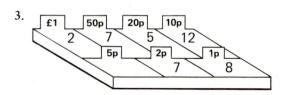

4.

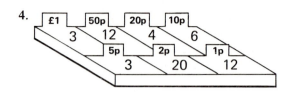

5.

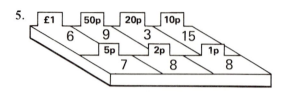

6.

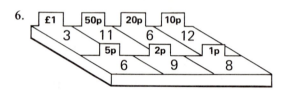

7.

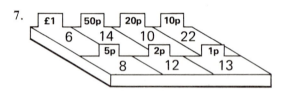

8.

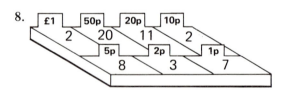

9.

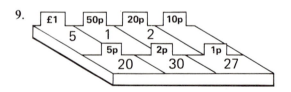

10.

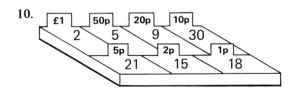

3.5   Money problems_____

You are in charge of the school shop.

A classmate buys something costing less than
£1 and gives you a one pound coin for it. You
give back the difference — this is called *change*.

Example 1

Priti has £1 to spend. She buys an item for
30p and gives you £1. How much change do
you give her back?

$$\text{Change} = £1 - 30p$$
$$= 100p - 30p$$
$$= 70p$$

Example 2

Tommy spends 57p at the shop. How much
change do you give him from £1. You want
to give him as few coins as possible. List the
coins which you should give him.

$$\text{Change} = £1 - 57p$$
$$= 43p$$

Coins given in change: 20p, 20p, 2p, 1p

Exercise 61

For each sum of money you are given £1. How much
change should you give?

1. 40p	2. 80p	3. 50p
4. 65p	5. 15p	6. 5p
7. 23p	8. 37p	9. 56p
10. 84p	11. 41p	12. 78p

For each sum of money you are given £5. How much
change should you give?

13. £2·60	14. £3·70	15. £4·90
16. £1·85	17. £3·25	18. £2·17
19. £1·09	20. £4·71	21. £2·48
22. 76p	23. £4·92	24. £1·11

For each of these sums spent at the tuck shop, your
classmates gives you £1. In each case, write down
how much change and which coins you would give
back.

25. 39p	26. 46p	27. 55p
28. 62p	29. 91p	30. 8p
31. 23p	32. 88p	33. 11p
34. 94p	35. 37p	36. 15p

For each of these amounts spent at the school shop,
your classmate gives you £5. In each case, write down
how much change and which coins you would give
them back?

37. £1·60	38. £2·50	39. £3·65
40. £1·75	41. £2·52	42. £1·61
43. £3·73	44. £4·01	45. 38p
46. £1·03	47. £1·35	48. £1·13

Example 3

How much will it cost to buy a box of
chocolates at £1·95 and a birthday card at
42p? How much change will you get from £5?

$$\text{Cost} = £1·95 + 42p$$
$$= £2·37$$

$$\text{Change} = £5 - £2·37$$
$$= £2·63$$

Exercise 62

How much will it cost to buy the following items?
1. An ice cream at 25p and a bar of chocolate at 18p.
2. A toy car at 65p, a lorry at £1·25 and a van at 99p.
3. A loaf of bread at 46p and six buns at 57p.
4. A transistor radio at £9.95 and four batteries
   at 84p.
5. A can of coke at 25p and a packet of crisps at 14p.
6. A toothbrush at 79p and a tube of toothpaste
   at 84p.
7. A Lego train at £14.95 and a box of rails at £3·85.
8. A doll at £2·75 and doll's clothes at £1·99.
9. A packet of washing powder at 88p and a bottle
   of fabric conditioner at 72p.
10. A packet of biscuits at 37p and a piece of cheese
    at 54p.

Write down the change you will be given from £1 for
these purchases.
11. A chicken sandwich at 62p.
12. A cup of coffee at 28p and a chocolate biscuit
    at 16p.
13. A ticket for a school concert at 75p and a
    programme at 15p.
14. A bowl of soup at 35p and a glass of milk at 18p.
15. A yogurt at 19p, a packet of biscuits at 28p and
    an apple at 12p.

Write down the change you will be given from £5 for these purchases.

16. A train ticket at £2·85 and a magazine at 65p.
17. Chicken noodle soup at 45p and a special fried rice at £2·30.
18. A pair of socks at £1·49 and a pair of gym shoes at £1·99.
19. A ticket to a football match at £1·50, a cup of tea at 20p and a pie at 45p.
20. A bunch of bananas at 75p, four apples at 46p and three oranges at 33p.

Exercise 63

1. Ali went into the newsagent and bought a comic for 25p and a magazine for 55p. How much did he spend?
2. Mum paid £12·95 for the months rental on the colour T.V. She handed over a £20 note. How much change did she get?
3. Jane has £4·20 in her purse. She buys her friend Diane a present for £2·89 and a birthday card for 35p. How much has she left in her purse?
4. Santosh saves £24·50 from his paper round and gets £12 from his father. With the money he buys a cassette player for £22·95. How much does he have left?
5. On the way home from the football match three friends went into a chip shop.

They bought a chicken supper, a pie supper and fish and chips. How much did they spend?

6. Mr. Smith bought a new car for £5650. The garage allowed him £2790 for his old car. How much did he have to pay?
7. The dress Fiona wanted to buy cost £33·95. She had only £28·84 in her purse. She decided to ask her mother for the extra money. How much did she ask her mother for?

8. Michael received £34·40 for his first week's wage. He gave £22·50 to his mother and bought a present for his father costing £2·95. How much money did he have left?
9. Patricia saw a pair of jeans that she liked in a shop. They were priced at £19·90, but she could not afford them. A week later the shop had a sale and the jeans were reduced to £14·95. How much did the shop take off the price?
10. The Jones family rented a car for their two week summer holiday. It cost £85·50 for the first week and £78·75 for the second week. What was the total cost of hiring the car?
11. Donald received £10 for his birthday. He spent £4·25 on a record and £2·65 on a teeshirt. How much of his birthday money did he have left?
12. The Trent family sold their terraced house for £36 750 and bought a semi-detached for £45 825. How much extra money did they need?
13. Alison bought a cat basket for £14·95 and a cat bowl for £1·75. How much change did she get from £20?
14. Here is Sandy's shopping list.

1 tin of beans	37p
1 packet of sausages	56p
half a dozen eggs	58p
1 tin of tomato soup	29p

How much does the shopping cost?
15. A book is published in two versions, the hardback at £12·95 and the paperback at £8·65. Mrs Mark buys one copy of each and the shop reduces the total cost by 75p. How much does Mrs Mark have to pay?
16. Mum, Dad, and Stuart go shopping in the Special Sale.

Mum buys a garden spade marked £7·95.
Dad buys a box of handkerchiefs marked 85p.
Stuart buys a toy car marked £1·85.
How much did each of them have to pay?

17. Andrew saved £150 to buy a computer. The computer costs £119·95. He bought a cassette recorder for £24·90, a computer game for £19·90 and two blank tapes for £1·20. Andrew did not have enough money and borrowed the rest from his father. How much money did Andrew have to borrow?

18. Mr O'Connor is trying to decide where to do his shopping. He sees adverts for two local stores. He writes down the information they tell him.

	ASDA	FINEFARE
TIN OF CATFOOD	38p	36p
PACKET OF DIGESTIVES	54p	57p
TUB OF MARGARINE	28p	24p
WASHING-UP LIQUID	59p	62p
TUBE OF TOOTHPASTE	46p	47p

Which store is offering the better bargain on all five items together?

19. Mrs Anderson, the newsagent, opens her shop in the morning. This diagram shows the money in her till.

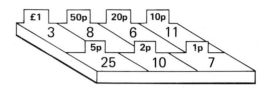

Her first customers buy newspapers for 22p. They each pay with a 50p piece. How many customers can Mrs Anderson serve before her change runs out?

20. Mr Sheen is a price watcher. He notes the prices of various items between November and April. Here are some details.

	November	April
Cauliflower	48p	66p
Tin of peas	24p	26p
Bag of potatoes	68p	59p
Dozen eggs	96p	96p

Decide whether the price of each item has increased or decreased. Calculate by how much the price of each has changed.

Investigation 3B

The Float

Look carefully at the table below.

Amount	50p	20p	10p	5p	2p	1p
1p						1
2p					1	
3p					1	1
⋮						
37p		1	1	1	1	
⋮						
84p	1	1	1		2	
⋮						
99p	1	2		1	2	

Now copy and complete the table for all amounts of money between 1p and 99p. In each case fill in the table so that the fewest coins possible are used.

A *float* is the amount of change allocated to a till at the beginning of a day's business.
A £10 float could be made up as follows:

5	£1 coins	= £ 5·00
6	50p coins	= £ 3·00
5	20p coins	= £ 1·00
5	10p coins	= 50p
5	5p coins	= 25p
10	2p coins	= 5p
	Total	= £10·00

1. Look at your table and suggest another way to make up a £10 float.
2. Suggest a way to make up a £5 float.
3. Suggest a way to make up a £20 float.
4. You run a newsagent's shop. You discover that most of your early morning customers buy newspapers in the price range 16p – 25p. Most customers pay with 50p coins. How would you make up the best float for this situation?

Investigation 3C

Floats and Giving Change

You run a newsagent's shop. In the morning you start with a £10 float?

1. How would you make it up?

Here are the details of the first 10 customers.

Customer	Bill	Coin offered by customer
1	24p	50p
2	22p	£1
3	35p	50p
4	62p	£1
5	24p	£1
6	33p	50p
7	22p	£1
8	25p	£1
9	21p	£1
10	18p	20p

2. Have you managed to give everyone the correct change?
3. How many coins of each kind have you now?
4. Continue the process for the next ten customers? They offer the same coins and receive the same change as the previous ten customers. Look at the details in the table on the left.
5. When did the till run out of change?
6. If it has not run out of change continue the process until it does run out of change?
7. Can you suggest a better way of making up the £10 float?
8. Test the new float against the customers above.
9. Whose float lasted the longest?
   Compare your results with the rest of the class.

4 Measure

4.1 Length — practical problems

To measure the length of objects you can use a ruler.
This ruler is marked in centimetres (cm) and half centimetres.

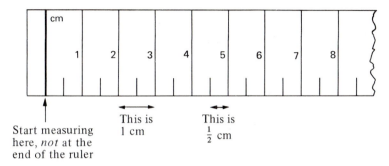

Start measuring
here, *not* at the
end of the ruler

This is
1 cm

This is
$\frac{1}{2}$ cm

Example 1

Find the length of these lines.

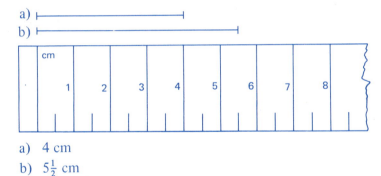

a) 4 cm

b) $5\frac{1}{2}$ cm

Most rules are marked in centimetres (cm) and millimetres (mm):

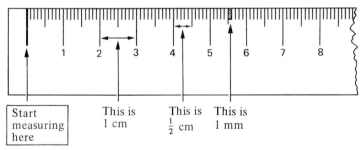

Start
measuring
here

This is
1 cm

This is
$\frac{1}{2}$ cm

This is
1 mm

Example 2

Find the length of these lines.

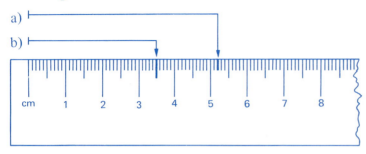

a) 5 cm 2 mm
b) 3 cm 5 mm or $3\frac{1}{2}$ cm

Exercise 64

Find the lengths of these lines.

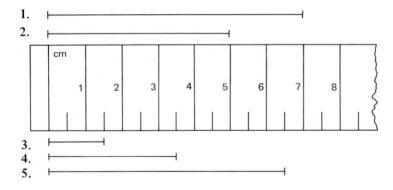

Find the length of these lines.

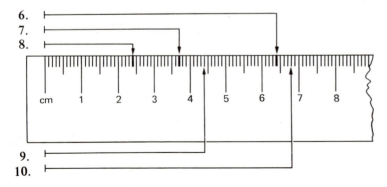

Use a ruler to measure the lengths of these lines.

11. ————————————————
12. ——————————
13. ————————————
14. —————————
15. ——————————————
16. ————————————————————
17. ————————
18. ————————————————
19. ————
20. ——————

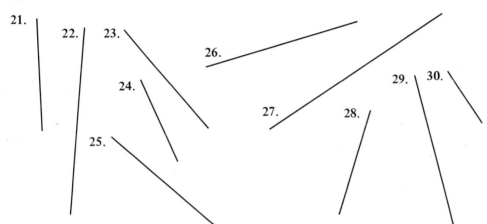

21.
22.   23.
24.
25.   26.
27.   28.
29.   30.

Exercise 65

In questions **1** to **10**, measure the length of each object shown.

1. The key   **2.** The pair of compasses

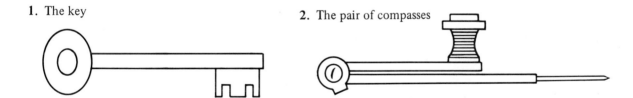

3. The screwdriver

4. The domino

5. The match   **6.** The nail

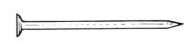

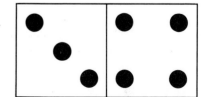

7. The paper clip

8. The pencil

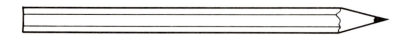

9. The rubber

10. The pair of pliers

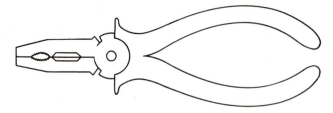

Example 3

Find the length of these lines.

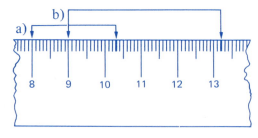

a)   2 cm 3 mm
b)   4 cm 2 mm

Exercise 66

Find the length of these lines.

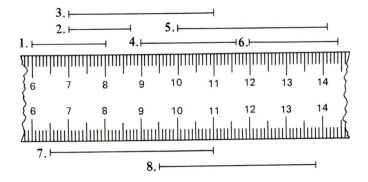

9. Look at the car and trailer below. Find the length of

    a) the car   b) the trailer
    c) the car and trailer coupled together

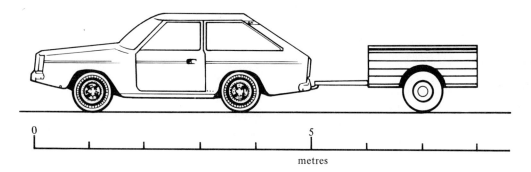

10. Look at the bungalow below. Find the width of

    a) the bungalow and garage   b) the garage only
    c) the bungalow only   d) the windows
    e) the front door   f) the garage door

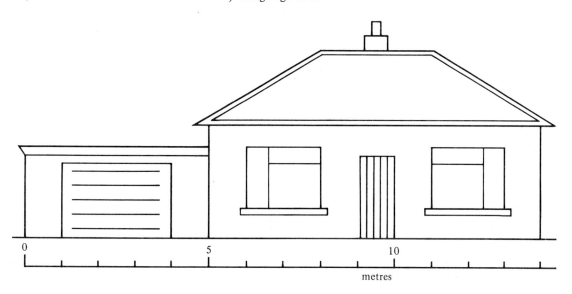

Exercise 67

For each question, draw a line of the length given:
  1. 6 cm   2. 5 cm   3. 2 cm
  4. 8 cm   5. 3 cm   6. 2 cm 5 mm
  7. 3 cm   8. 5 cm 3 mm   9. 6 cm 8 mm
10. 8 cm 9 mm

Swop Maths books with your neighbour.
Check each other's work.

For each question, draw a line of the length given:
11. 7 cm   12. $3\frac{1}{2}$ cm   13. $5\frac{1}{2}$ cm
14. 4 cm 3 mm   15. 6 cm 1 mm   16. 8 cm 3 mm
17. 2 cm 9 mm   18. 1 cm 6 mm   19. 3 cm 8 mm
20. 7 mm

Swop Maths books with your neighbour.
Check each other's work.

If you want to measure short lengths use
centimetre (cm) and millimetre (mm). For
greater distances, use metres (m) or kilometres
(km)

$$1 \text{ km} = 1000 \text{ m}$$
$$1 \text{ m} = 100 \text{ cm}$$
$$1 \text{ cm} = 10 \text{ mm}$$

To measure the width of a pencil we use
millimetres.

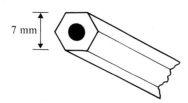

7 mm

To measure the length of this book use
centimetres.

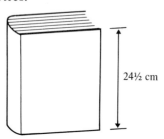

24½ cm

To measure the height of a mountain we use
metres.

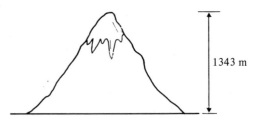

1343 m

To measure distances between towns we use
kilometres.

Inverness

555 km

Leeds

Exercise 68

Write down the best unit to use when you measure:
  1. the length of a fly
  2. the width of a fridge
  3. the length of a swimming pool
  4. the distance to the moon
  5. your height
  6. the thickness of a book
  7. the distance to London
  8. the height of a washing machine
  9. the length of a lorry
10. the thickness of a sheet of metal

11. the length of an aircraft
12. the height of a flower
13. the distance you travel to school
14. the width of a model aeroplane
15. the length of an oil pipe line
16. the height of an oak tree
17. the length of wire needed to fence in a field
18. the depth of a puddle
19. the height of the Tower of London
20. the height of a satellite above the Earth

There are many different instruments for
measuring lengths.

A ruler measures in cm and mm, up to 30 cm.

A metre rule measures in cm and mm, up to
1 metre.

A short tape measures in cm and mm, up
to 150 cms.

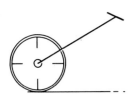

A long tape measures in cm and m, up to
20 metres.

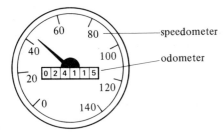

A trundle wheel measures in metres.

An odometer or tripmeter measures in km
or miles.

Exercise 69

Which instrument would you use to measure

1. the width of your Maths book,
2. the height of the classroom,
3. the length of the corridor,
4. the width of the football pitch,
5. the distance round the school,
6. the distance from Liverpool to Bristol,
7. the length of a staple,
8. the width of the blackboard,
9. the height of your chair,
10. the distance round the classroom?

Exercise 70

Choose a suitable instrument and measure

1. the width of this book
2. the length and breadth of your desk
3. the height of the door
4. your height
5. the length of your hand
6. the height of your desk
7. the length of the classroom
8. the length of the corridor
9. the width of the hockey pitch
10. the distance round the school building.

11. the length of your foot
12. the length of your arm from the elbow to the tip of your fingers
13. the length of your leg from the top of your knee to your heel
14. the circumference or the distance around a tree
15. the distance from the school gate to the nearest door of the school
16. the circumference of your head
17. the distance between the uprights of the goal posts
18. the distance between the tips of your fingers with with your arms stretched out
19. the width of various coins
20. the width of the blackboard.

4.2   The metric system — LENGTH

```
10 mm = 1 cm
100 cm  = 1 m
1000 m   = 1 km
```

Example 1

a) Change 160 millimetres (mm) to centimetres (cm).

b) Change 4 kilometres (km) to metres (m).

c) Change 275 centimetres (cm) to metres and centimetres.

a) 160 mm = (160 ÷ 10) cm = 16 cm

b) 4 km   = (4 × 1000) m = 4000 m

c) 275 cm = (275 ÷ 100) m
            = 2·75 m or 2 m 75 cm

Exercise 71

Change

1. 190 mm, to cm	**2.** 930 mm, to cm
3. 60 mm, to cm	**4.** 700 mm, to cm
5. 7 cm, to mm	**6.** 16 cm, to mm
7. 28 cm, to mm	**8.** 40 cm, to mm
9. 720 cm, to m	**10.** 51 800 cm, to m
11. 65 000 cm, to m	**12.** 80 000 cm, to m
13. 4000 cm, to m	**14.** 37 000 cm, to m
15. 8 m, to cm	**16.** 45 m, to cm
17. 236 m, to cm	**18.** 320 m, to cm
19. 500 m, to cm	**20.** 39 m, to cm
21. 79 km, to m	**22.** 137 km, to m
23. 50 km , to m	**24.** 290 km, to m
25. 100 km, to m	**26.** 42 000 m, to km
27. 215 000 m, to km	**28.** 80 000 m, to km
29. 460 000 m, to km	**30.** 300 000 m, to km

31. 215 cm, to m and cm	**32.** 632 cm, to m
33. 304 cm, to m	**34.** 1595 m, to km and m
35. 4326 m, to km and m	**36.** 2350 m, to km
37. 3400 m, to km	**38.** 5076 m, to km
39. 54 mm, to cm and mm	**40.** 79 mm, to cm
41. 8 cm 6 mm, to mm	**42.** 9 cm 8 mm, to mm
43. 1 m 45 cm, to cm	**44.** 3 m 72 cm, to cm
45. 5 m 7 cm, to cm	**46.** 1 km 870 m, to m
47. 2 km 58 m, to m	**48.** 3 km 58 m, to m
49. 4 km 80 m, to m	**50.** 1 km 5 m, to m

51. ½ cm, to mm	**52.** ½ m, to cm
53. ½ km, to m	**54.** ¼ m, to cm
55. ¼ km, to m	**56.** 1½ cm, to mm
57. 2¾ m, to cm	**58.** 3½ km, to m
59. 4¼ m, to cm	**60.** 2¾ km, to m

Example 2

a) Add together 3 mm, 5 mm, and 8 mm. Give the answer in cm and mm.

b) Find the sum of 4 cm 7 mm, 6 cm 3 mm, and 2 cm 9 mm.

c) Find the sum of 3 m 65 cm, 2 m 8 cm and 1 m 70 cm.

a) 3 mm + 5 mm + 8 mm = 16 mm
                        or 1 cm 6 mm
                        or 1·6 cm

b)
cm	mm		cm
4	7		4·7
6	3	or	6·3
2	9		2·9
13	9		13·9

Answer: 13 cm 9 mm or 13·9 cm

c)
m	cm		m
3	65		3·65
2	08	or	2·08
1	70		1·70
7	43		7·43

Answer: 7 m 43 cm or 7·43 m

Exercise 72

Add the following.

1. 2 mm, 8 mm, 9 mm	**2.** 3 mm, 5 mm, 6 mm
3. 9 mm, 6 mm, 8 mm	**4.** 53 cm, 35 cm, 41 cm
5. 46 cm, 37 cm, 63 cm	**6.** 27 cm, 36 cm, 55 cm
7. 334 m, 221 m, 713 m	**8.** 403 m, 626 m, 545 m
9. 824 m, 253 m, 65 m	**10.** 953 m, 36 m, 75 m

Find the sum for each part of the question, then state which is the 'odd answer out'.

11. a) 3 mm, 8 mm, 7 mm
b) 5 mm, 6 mm, 8 mm
c) 4 mm, 5 mm, 9 mm
d) 1 mm, 9 mm, 8 mm

12. a) 25 cm, 31 cm, 20 cm, 53 cm
b) 42 cm, 12 cm, 71 cm, 4 cm
c) 35 cm, 17 cm, 64 cm, 23 cm
d) 50 cm, 37 cm, 13 cm, 29 cm

13. a) 451 m, 332 m, 542 m
b) 270 m, 651 m, 404 m
c) 534 m, 705 m, 86 m
d) 217 m, 865 m, 233 m

Find the sum for each question

14. 3 cm 5 mm, 2 cm 1 mm, 1 cm 3 mm
15. 2·3 cm, 1·4 cm, 3·5 cm
16. 4·6 cm, 1·4 cm, 3·5 cm
17. 4 m 42 cm, 1 m 21 cm, 2 m 13 cm
18. 3 m 45 cm, 1 m 16 cm, 5 m 23 cm
19. 1·81 m, 3·63 m, 4·18 m
20. 2 km 235 m, 1 km 182 m, 5 km 335 m
21. 3 km 416 m, 2 km 523 m, 3 km 345 m
22. 1·504 km, 3·174 km, 2·667 km
23. 1·525 km, 1·163 km, 1·368 km

Find the sum for each part of the question, then state which is the 'odd answer out'.

24. a) 4 cm 6 mm, 3 cm 5 mm, 1 cm 4 mm
b) 2 cm 3 mm, 1 cm 7 mm, 5 cm 6 mm
c) 3·8 cm, 2·7 cm, 3 cm
d) 6 cm 3 mm, 2·4 cm, 8 mm

25. a) 1 m 52 cm, 2 m 31 cm, 3 m 42 cm
b) 4·23 m, 1·78 m, 1·24 m
c) 2 m 17 cm, 1·32 m, 3 m 76 cm
d) 1·59 m, 1·30 m, 4 m 46 cm

26. a) 2 km 542 m, 1 km 235 m, 3 km 473 m
b) 1 km 816 m, 1 km 334 m, 4 km
c) 2·257 km, 4·361 km, 0·532 km
d) 6·151 km, 913 m, 0·086 km

27. a) 4 km 265 m, 3 km 113 m, 2 km 72 m
b) 5·394 km, 1 km 32 m, 3·024 km
c) 2 km 193 m, 2·151 km, 5 km 6 m
d) 1·364 km, 6 km 82 m, 2 km 4 m

Example 3

Find the difference between 2 cm and 1 cm 4 mm.

The difference is $(2 \text{ cm}) - (1 \text{ cm } 4 \text{ mm})$
$$= 20 \text{ mm} - 14 \text{ mm}$$
$$= 6 \text{ mm}$$

Example 4

a) Subtract 2 cm 8 mm from 4 cm 2 mm.
b) Subtract 1 km 78 m from 2 km 5 m.

a)	cm	mm		cm
	4	2		4·2
−	2	8	or	− 2·8
	1	4		1·4

Answer: 1 cm 4 mm or 1·4 cm

b)	km	m		km
	2	005		2·005
−	1	078	or	1·078
	0	927		0·927

Answer: 927 m or 0·927 km

Exercise 73

Find the difference between:

1. 5 cm and 4 cm 6 mm   **2.** 3 cm and 2 cm 7 mm
3. 3 cm and 1·4 cm   **4.** 5 cm and 1·8 cm
5. 4 m and 3 m 56 cm   **6.** 2 m and 1 m 72 cm
7. 6 m and 2·35 m   **8.** 5 m and 1·40 m
9. 8 m and 3 m 4 cm   **10.** 6 km and 5 km 750 m

11. 5 km and 3·645 km   **12.** 7 km and 3·826 km
13. 4 km and 2 km 68 m   **14.** 6 km and 2 km 40 m
15. 6 km and 2 km 5 m   **16.** 9 km and 2 km 925 m
17. 3 cm and 8 mm   **18.** 3 m and 7 cm
19. 2 km and 6 m   **20.** 1 m and 850 mm

Subtract for each part of the question, then state which is the 'odd answer out'.

21. a) 2 cm 3 mm from 5 cm 8 mm
    b) 3·7 cm from 7·2 cm
    c) 5 cm 9 mm from 9 cm 6 mm

22. a) 6 cm 4 mm from 8·9 cm
    b) 1·6 cm from 4 cm 3 mm
    c) 7 cm from 9 cm 7 mm

23. a) 6 m 54 cm from 9 m 79 cm
    b) 2·47 m from 5·82 m
    c) 5 m 35 cm from 8·6 m

24. a) 1 m 8 cm from 3·63 m
    b) 3·61 m from 6 m 6 cm
    c) 2 m 5 cm from 4 m 60 cm

25. a) 5 km 152 m from 7 km 487 m
    b) 3·328 km from 5·673 km
    c) 1 km 594 m from 3 km 939 m

26. a) 3 km 7 m from 6·591 km
    b) 248 m from 3·822 km
    c) 683 m from 4 km 257 m

Exercise 74

1. On Saturday Kate knitted 15 cm of her new jumper. On Sunday she knitted another 20 cm. How much did she knit in those two days?
2. Helen cycled 23 kilometres in the morning and 18 km in the afternoon. How far did she cycle?
3. A digger has to excavate an 85 m long trench. By lunchtime 28 m had been dug. How many metres had still to be dug?
4. On one day the rainfall measured 18 mm. If 6 mm fell in the first 18 hours, how much fell in the last 6 hours?
5. Mr Jones buys 4 m of curtain material for his window. He only needs 3m 76 cm. How much material has he left over?
6. A 2 metre post is driven into the ground. If 1 m 62 cm is above the ground, how much of the post is below the ground?

7.

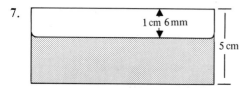

What is the depth of the liquid in the tank?

8. Pine Grove is 654 m long. Beech Grove is 497 m long. Elm Grove is 960 m long. How far does Tracy have to walk to school? Give your answer in kilometres and metres.

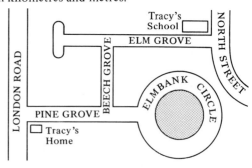

9. What is the diameter of the hole in this washer?

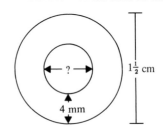

10. Find the length of the spade in metres.

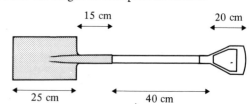

11. Find the height of the clock tower.

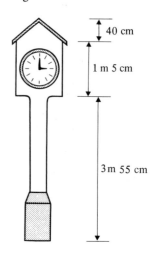

12. Find the height of the chimney top from the ground.

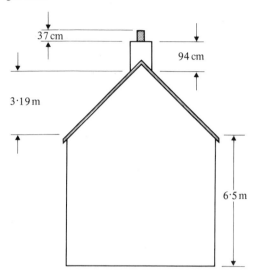

13. I have to make a picture frame like the one illustrated.

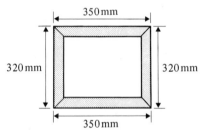

I have a piece of wood which is 1 metre in length. Can I use this piece of wood for making three sides of the picture frame? Which three sides can I make?

14. Workmen have to erect 6 km of fencing in 4 days. During the first three days the workmen erect 1 km 240 m, 1 km 376 m and 1 km 485 m respectively. How much fencing has to be erected on the fourth day?

15. "Here's Hoping" was racing a distance of 4 km 350 m. After 3 km 685 m he fell at the Water Jump. How far was he from the winning post?

16. A double-glazed window is made up of two sheets of 4 mm thick glass and a 6 mm space in between. How thick is the window? Give your answer in cm and mm.

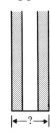

17. What length of wood is needed to make this gate?

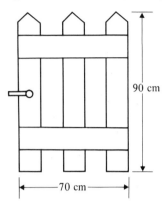

The wood is only sold in one-metre lengths. How many lengths must be bought? What length of wood is left over?

18. A man has a 10-metre ball of string which he uses for fastening three parcels.

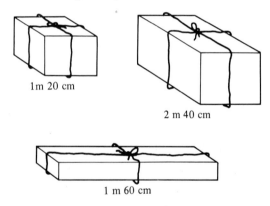

1m 20 cm

2 m 40 cm

1 m 60 cm

The lengths required are shown. How much string will be left on the ball?

19. A man buys a 5-metre length of curtain track for these two windows.

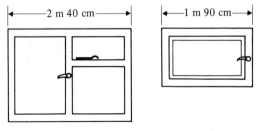

He cuts off 2 lengths to fit the windows. What length of track will be left over?

4.3   The metric system — MASS

The units of mass which are commonly used
for weighing objects are the gram, the kilogram
and the tonne.

1000 grams (g)   = 1 kilogram (kg)
1000 kilograms (kg) = 1 tonne (t)

The gram is a very small mass.

A sugar lump
weighs about 5 g.

A plastic bucket
full of water
weighs about 10 kg.

An apple weighs
about 100 g.

An electric cooker
weighs about 50 kg.

This weight is too
heavy for most
people to lift.

A full bottle of
milk weighs
about 1 kg.

An ordinary car for
4 passengers weighs
about 1 t.

An ocean liner
weighs about 60 000 t

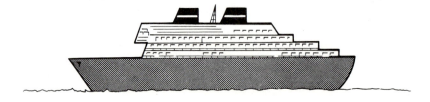

Exercise 75

Look at the above examples, then give the most sensible unit for measuring the mass of each of the following.

1. A cotton reel	2. A sack of potatoes	11. Yourself	12. An orange
3. A ball pen	4. A lorry	13. An elephant	14. A mouse
5. A light bulb	6. A television set	15. A notebook	16. A submarine
7. A large bunch of bananas	8. An aeroplane	17. A sheep	18. A letter
9. A full bottle of ink	10. A bicycle	19. An egg	20. A washing machine.

Example 1

Change the following as indicated.

a) 3000 g, to kg   b) 6 t, to kg
c) 2 kg 625 g, to g   d) 7250 kg, to t

a) 3000 g = (3000 ÷ 1000) kg = 3 kg
b) 6 t = (6 × 1000) kg = 6000 kg
c) 2 kg 625 g = (2 × 1000) g + 625 g
= 2625 g
d) 7250 kg = (7250 ÷ 1000) t = 7·25 t

Exercise 76

Change the following as indicated.

1. 5000 g, to kg
2. 12 000 g, to kg
3. 36 000 g, to kg
4. 40 000 g, to kg
5. 3000 kg, to t
6. 15 000 kg, to t
7. 27 000 kg, to t
8. 30 000 kg, to t
9. 2500 g, to kg and g
10. 7500 kg, to t and kg

11. 2 kg, to g
12. 6 kg, to g
13. 10 kg, to g
14. 24 kg, to g
15. 1 t, to kg
16. 9 t, to kg
17. 20 t, to kg
18. 37 t, to kg
19. 1 kg 750 g, to g
20. 2 t 250 kg, to kg

21. 2250 g, to kg and g
22. 3750 g, to kg
23. 2520 g, to kg and g
24. 8075 g, to kg
25. 3 kg 450 g, to g
26. 5 kg 80 g, to g

Example 2

Add the following.

a) 370 g, 465 g, 630 g
b) 1 t 75 kg, 2 t 350 kg, 1 t 50 kg, 850 kg

a) 370 g + 465 g + 630 g = 1465 g
= 1 kg 465 g
= 1·465 kg

b)

t	kg	t
1	75	1·075
2	350	2·350
1	50	1·050
+ 0	850	0·850
5	325	5·325

Answer: 5 t 325 kg or 5·325 t

Exercise 77

Add the following.

1. 450 g, 600 g, 570 g
2. 270 g, 650 g, 880 g
3. 325 g, 762 g, 800 g
4. 572 g, 694 g, 878 g
5. 62 g, 87 g, 69 g
6. 880 kg, 760 kg
7. 430 kg, 650 kg, 810 kg
8. 545 kg, 694 kg, 738 kg
9. 85 kg, 79 kg, 96 kg
10. 641 kg, 877 kg, 964 kg

11. 1 kg 750 g, 2 kg 500 g
12. 2·340 kg, 1·720 kg, 2·390 kg
13. 3 kg 650 g, 2 kg 480 g, 1 kg 70 g
14. 2 kg 40 g, 3 kg 70 g, 1 kg 80 g
15. 1 kg 7 g, 2 kg 8 g, 3 kg 9 g
16. 2 t 500 kg, 1 t 800 kg
17. 3 t 680 kg, 2 t 210 kg, 1 t 425 kg
18. 1·960 t, 2·620 t, 90 kg
19. 2 t 85 kg, 2·017 t, 1 t 53 kg
20. 3·005 t, 2 t 512 kg, 3 t 84 kg

Find the sum for each part of the question, then state which is the 'odd answer out'.

21. a) 2 kg 375 g, 4 kg 480 g, 1 kg 765 g
b) 3·250 kg, 2·787 kg, 2·565 kg
c) 5 kg 163 g, 2 kg 382 g, 1 kg 75 g

22. a) 1 kg 65 g, 560 g, 1·472 kg
b) 1 kg 34 g, 1 kg 55 g, 1 kg 8 g
c) 1·109 kg, 650 g, 2·211 kg

23. a) 767 kg, 878 kg, 575 kg
b) 1 t 8 kg, 1 t 14 kg
c) 1·214 t, 428 kg, 578 kg

24. a) 3·462 t, 4·504 t, 2·794 t
b) 549 kg, 485 kg, 42 kg
c) 348 kg, 1 t 12 kg, 9 t 400 kg

25. a) 2 t 49 kg, 3·720 t, 890 kg
b) 3 t 72 kg, 1·952 t, 1634 kg
c) 4 t 93 kg, 0·798 t, 1768 kg

26. a) 8·001 t, 3 t 247 kg, 3 t 762 kg
b) 7·213 t, 5 t 463 kg, 2324 kg
c) 7 t 3 kg, 6·989 t, 1·008 t

Example 3

a) Find the difference between 2 tonnes and 1 t 450 kg.

b) Subtract 1 kg 85 g from 3 kg 4 g.

a)   t   kg   t

     2   000   or   2·000

  − 1   450   − 1·450

     0   550   0·550

Answer: 550 kg or 0·550 t

b)   kg   g   kg

     3   004   or   3·004

  − 1   085   − 1·085

     1   919   1·919

Answer: 1 kg 919 g or 1·919 kg

Exercise 78

Find the difference between

1. 1 kg and 400 g
2. 1 kg and 650 g
3. 1 kg and 75 g
4. 1 kg and 9 g
5. 3 kg 460 g and 1 kg 276 g
6. 2 kg 87 g and 1 kg 350 g
7. 12·700 kg and 9·800 kg
8. 10·760 kg and 3·970 kg
9. 2 kg 74 g and 1 kg 86 g
10. 3 kg 8 g and 1 kg 9 g

11. 1 t and 840 kg
12. 1 t and 60 kg
13. 1 t and 4 kg
14. 2 t 60 kg and 1 t 500 kg
15. 2·540 t and 1·762 t
16. 3 t 80 kg and 2 t 95 kg
17. $15\frac{1}{2}$ t and 10 t 800 kg
18. $3\frac{1}{4}$ t and 1 t 680 kg
19. 4 t 50 kg and $2\frac{3}{4}$ t
20. 2 t 40 kg and 1 t 85 kg

Exercise 79

1. Tom Cook bought 1 kg of margarine. He used 250 g to make scones and 200 g to make pancakes. How much margarine did he have left?
2. Louise buys a bag of sweets. The bag says 'net weight 150 g including wrappers'. Louise collects the wrappers and weighs them The mass of the wrappers is 17 g. What is the mass of the sweets?

3. A lorry weighs 2·350 t empty.

How much can the lorry carry and still be allowed to cross the bridge?

4. The mass of an empty lorry is 3 t 70 kg. Fully loaded its mass is 26 t 14 kg. What is the mass of the load?

5. What is the usual mass of the contents of the packet below?

6. Mr Tubman goes on a slimming diet. Before he starts, he weighs 86·450 kg. During the first few days of his diet he loses 850 g, 740 g, 230 g, and 180 g respectively. How much does he weigh at the end of the fourth day?
7. I am going on holiday My two empty cases weigh 1 kg 370 g and 1 kg 750 g. On my air flight, I am allowed 20 kg of luggage including the cases. What is the largest mass I can add to the two cases?
8. A coal merchant received 20 tonnes of wet coal. After the coal had dried out the merchant put it into 50 kg bags. He discovered he was 1½ bags short. What was the mass of coal in the original 20 tonnes?

Investigation 4

1. Estimate the length and mass of each kind of transport below:

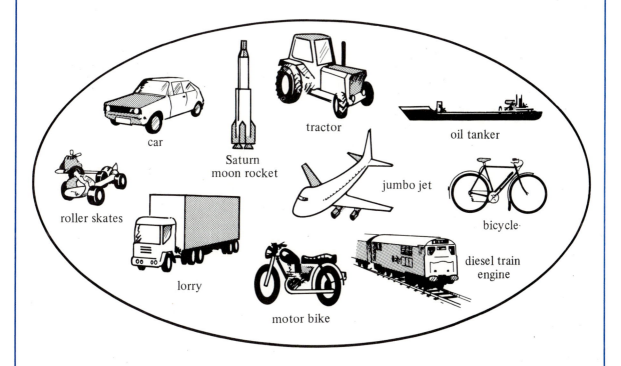

car

Saturn
moon rocket

tractor

oil tanker

roller skates

jumbo jet

bicycle

lorry

motor bike

diesel train
engine

Make two lists:
The first list should be in order of *length*
The second list should be in order of *mass*
Write your estimates of length and mass next to the items in the lists.

2. Make a list of:
 a) ten animals, birds, and insects
 b) ten objects
 Try to make the things in your lists as different from each other as possible.
 Estimate the length and mass of each thing. Write down each list in order of:
  (i) length
  (ii) mass

 Next to each thing in your lists, write your estimates of length and mass.

3. Check your answers using library reference books or other
 sources of information.

5 Shapes

5.1 Angles

An *angle* is the way we measure turn or change of direction.

When the wind changes direction, the weather vane turns to show the new wind direction.

When a door opens, it turns about its hinges.

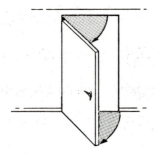

When a child plays on a swing, the swing chain turns . . .

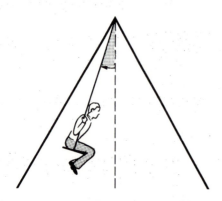

When the minute hand on a clock goes from ten past nine to twenty past nine, it turns through ten minutes.

In each case the amount of turn has been shaded in. This is called the angle.

A complete turn is divided into 360 parts called degrees.

1 complete turn = 360°

1 turn clockwise

1 turn anti-clockwise

A half turn = 180°

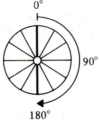

A half turn
clockwise

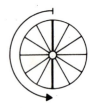

A half turn
anti-clockwise

A quarter turn = 90°

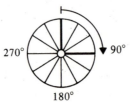

A quarter turn
clockwise

A quarter turn
anti-clockwise

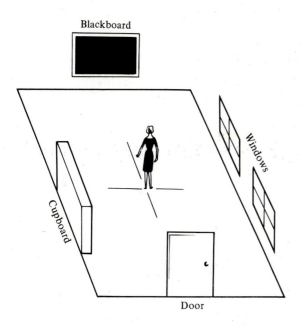

Blackboard

Windows

Cupboard

Door

David is facing the windows. What will he be facing if:
9. he turns through 180°
10. he does a quarter turn clockwise
11. he does a three quarter turn clockwise
12. he does a quarter turn anti-clockwise?

Ethel is facing the cupboard. What will she be facing if:
13. she turns through 90° clockwise
14. she turns through 270° clockwise
15. she turns through 360°
16. she turns through 180°?

Mohammed is facing the door. What will he be facing if:
17. he turns through 270° anti-clockwise
18. he turns through 90° anti-clockwise
19. he turns through 180°
20. he turns through 270° clockwise?

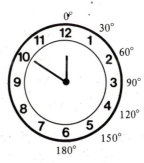

Example 1

Amanda is standing in the middle of the classroom – look at the picture above – facing the blackboard. What will she be facing if
  a) she turns half way round,
  b) she turns 90° clockwise?

  a) If Amanda turns half way round she will face the door.
  b) A 90° turn is a quarter turn. After a quarter turn clockwise Amanda will face the windows.

Exercise 80

For questions 1 to 20, look again at the picture of the classroom.

Amanda is facing the blackboard. What will she be facing if:
1. she does a quarter turn clockwise
2. she turns through 180°
3. she makes a complete turn
4. she does a quarter turn anti-clockwise?

Brian is facing the door. What will he be facing if:
5. he does a half turn
6. he turns through 90° clockwise
7. he turns through 360°
8. he does a quarter turn anti-clockwise?

When the hour hand moves from 12 o'clock to 1 o'clock, it goes through one-third of 90°.

$$\tfrac{1}{3} \text{ of } 90° = 30°$$

When the hour hand moves from 12 o'clock to 4 o'clock, it goes through

$$4 \times 30° = 120°$$

Exercise 81

How many degrees does the hour hand go through between:
1. 12 o'clock and 2 o'clock
2. 12 o'clock and 5 o'clock
3. 12 o'clock and 6 o'clock
4. 3 o'clock and 6 o'clock
5. 3 o'clock and 4 o'clock
6. 3 o'clock and 5 o'clock
7. 6 o'clock and 10 o'clock
8. 6 o'clock and 12 o'clock
9. 7 o'clock and 10 o'clock
10. 8 o'clock and 12 o'clock?

How many degrees does the *minute* hand go through between:

11. 5·00 and 5·20	**12.** 7·00 and 7·30
13. 8·00 and 8·15	**14.** 6·00 and 6·25
15. 10·00 and 10·05	**16.** 10·10 and 10·30
17. 8·15 and 8·25	**18.** 8·35 and 8·50
19. 1·20 and 1·45	**20.** 2·35 and 2·45

21. 7·00 and 7·45	**22.** 2·00 and 2·35
23. 3·00 and 3·40	**24.** 5·00 and 5·50
25. 8·00 and 9·00	**26.** 10.00 and 10·55
27. 5·10 and 5·45	**28.** 11·15 and 11·55
29. 2·25 and 3·00	**30.** 3·05 and 3·45

31. 8·00 and 8·01	**32.** 9·00 and 9·02
33. 11·00 and 11·12	**34.** 1·00 and 1·22
35. 2·00 and 2·09	**36.** 8·00 and 8·16
37. 7·04 and 7·24	**38.** 9·05 and 9·32
39. 3·14 and 3·42	**40.** 4·12 and 4·51?

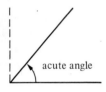
right angle

An angle of 90° is called a *right angle*.

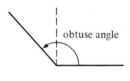
acute angle

An angle which is less than 90° is called an *acute angle*.

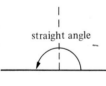
obtuse angle

An angle which is greater than 90° but less than 180° is called an *obtuse angle*.

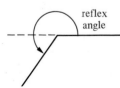
straight angle

An angle of 180° is called a *straight angle* because it makes a straight line.

reflex angle

An angle which is greater than 180° is called a *reflex angle*.

Exercise 82

In questions **1** to **6**, write down the kind of each angle shown.

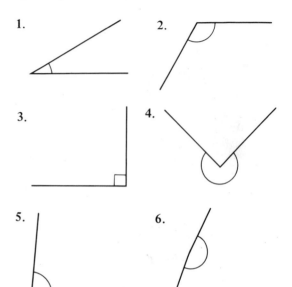

1.
2.
3.
4.
5.
6.

Draw the following angles:

7. a right angle
8. an obtuse angle greater than 120°
9. a reflex angle less than 270°
10. an acute angle less than 30°

Write down what kind of angles you can find in each of these pictures.

11. A brick wall

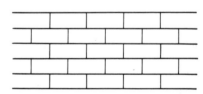

12. A diamond

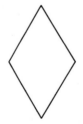

13. A honeycomb
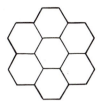

14. A door
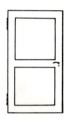

15. A star

16. A church window

17. What kind of doors open through 180°?
18. What kind of doors move through 360°?
19. What kind of doors open without moving through any angle?
20. Draw an object with acute, right, and obtuse angles. Label the angles clearly on your drawing.

An angle is made up of a vertex or corner and two arms going out from the vertex.

An angle is given a name using three different capital letters.
The first letter must be on one arm.
The middle letter must be the vertex.
The last letter must be on the other arm.

This is the angle PQR. The vertex Q is given a 'hat' to indicate an angle.

An angle can have more than one name. The angle at vertex A may be called:

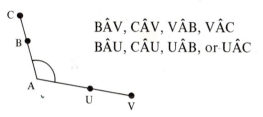

$\quad$ BÂV, CÂV, VÂB, VÂC
$\quad$ BÂU, CÂU, UÂB, or UÂC

Example 2

Using three letters, name the angles marked
i) a ii) b iii) c.

i) $\hat{a} = Q\hat{R}S$
ii) $\hat{b} = P\hat{M}S$
iii) $\hat{c} = Q\hat{P}R$ or $Q\hat{P}M$

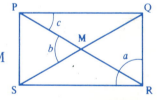

Exercise 83

Using three letters, name the marked angle or angles in each of the following diagrams:

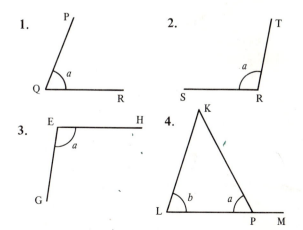

5.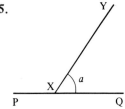

6.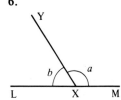

7.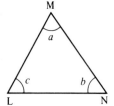

8.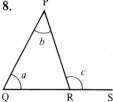

9.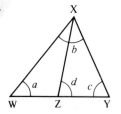

10.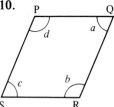

11.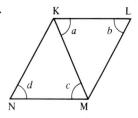

12.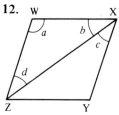

13.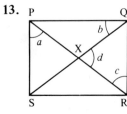

14.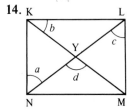

15.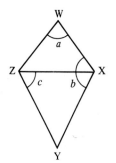

16.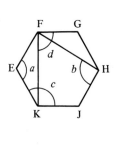

17.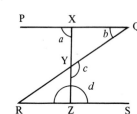

18.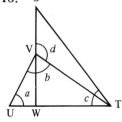

In the following examples state which are correct ways of naming the angle marked a.

19.
i) $J\hat{N}H$ ii) $G\hat{J}N$
iii) $K\hat{J}N$ iv) $N\hat{J}H$
v) $J\hat{G}N$ vi) $N\hat{J}G$

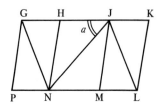

20.
i) $P\hat{V}X$ ii) $X\hat{V}W$
iii) $Q\hat{V}W$ iv) $W\hat{V}U$
v) $W\hat{V}P$ vi) $W\hat{V}X$
vii) $U\hat{V}X$ viii) $X\hat{V}Q$

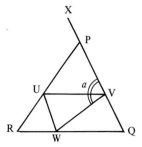

5.2 The protractor

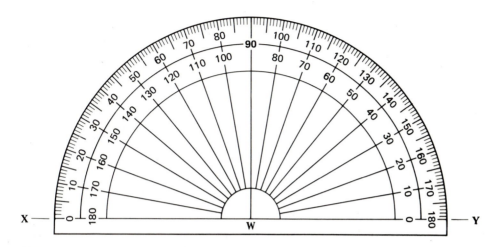

To measure an angle you need a protractor as shown above. **XY** shows the base line and **W** the centre point.

Example 1

Measure the size of **PQ̂R**

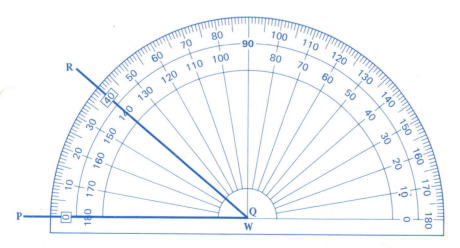

1. Place the protractor on the angle so that **W** is on **Q** as shown and **WX** lies on **PQ**.

2. Where the line **QR** cuts the scale, read off the angle on the scale starting from 0° at **P**

3. **PQ̂R** = 40°.

Example 2

Measure the size of LM̂N

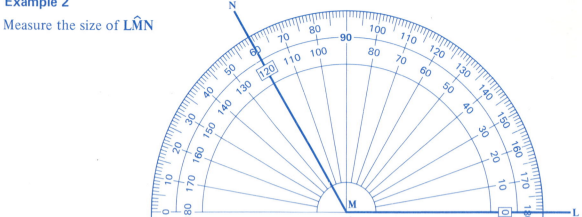

1. Place the protractor on the angle so that **W** is on **M** as shown and **WY** lies on **ML**.
2. Where the line **MN** cuts the scale, read off the angle on the scale starting from 0° at **L**.
3. **LM̂N** = 120°.

Exercise 84

For each question look at the diagram, then copy and fill in the details below.

1.

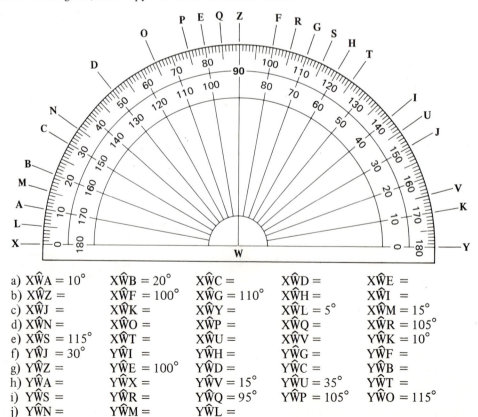

a) XŴA = 10°	XŴB = 20°	XŴC =	XŴD =	XŴE =
b) XŴZ =	XŴF = 100°	XŴG = 110°	XŴH =	XŴI =
c) XŴJ =	XŴK =	XŴY =	XŴL = 5°	XŴM = 15°
d) XŴN =	XŴO =	XŴP =	XŴQ =	XŴR = 105°
e) XŴS = 115°	XŴT =	XŴU =	XŴV =	YŴK = 10°
f) YŴJ = 30°	YŴI =	YŴH =	YŴG =	YŴF =
g) YŴZ =	YŴE = 100°	YŴD =	YŴC =	YŴB =
h) YŴA =	YŴX =	YŴV = 15°	YŴU = 35°	YŴT =
i) YŴS =	YŴR =	YŴQ = 95°	YŴP = 105°	YŴO = 115°
j) YŴN =	YŴM =	YŴL =		

2.

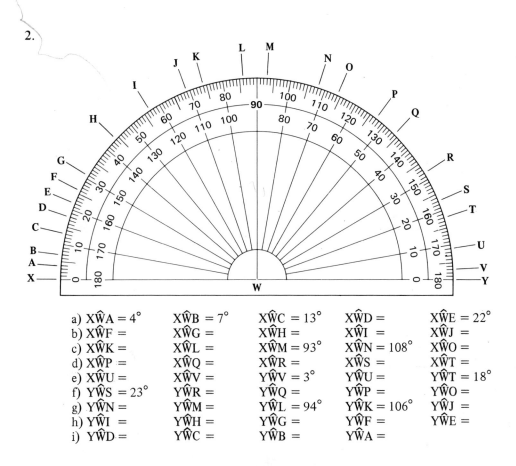

a) XŴA = 4° XŴB = 7° XŴC = 13° XŴD = XŴE = 22°
b) XŴF = XŴG = XŴH = XŴI = XŴJ =
c) XŴK = XŴL = XŴM = 93° XŴN = 108° XŴO =
d) XŴP = XŴQ = XŴR = XŴS = XŴT =
e) XŴU = XŴV = YŴV = 3° YŴU = YŴT = 18°
f) YŴS = 23° YŴR = YŴQ = YŴP = YŴO =
g) YŴN = YŴM = YŴL = 94° YŴK = 106° YŴJ =
h) YŴI = YŴH = YŴG = YŴF = YŴE =
i) YŴD = YŴC = YŴB = YŴA =

Exercise 85

With a protractor, measure each of the following angles.

1.

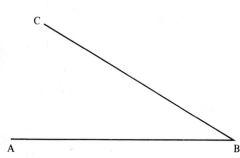

2.

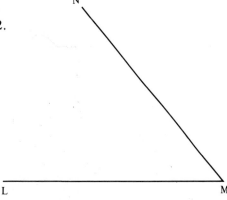

3.

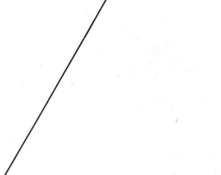

4.

5.

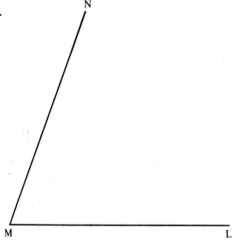

6.

7.

8.

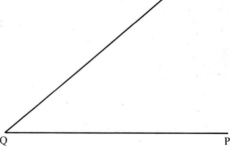

9.

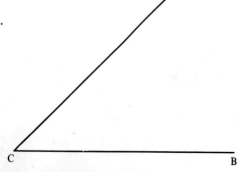

10.

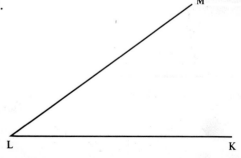

11.

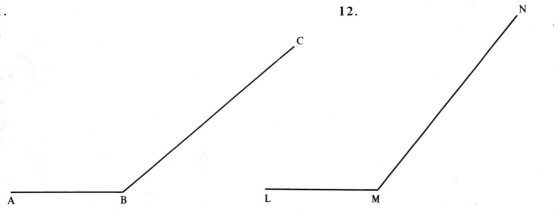

12.

13.

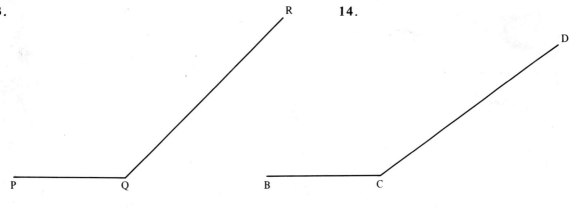

14.

15.

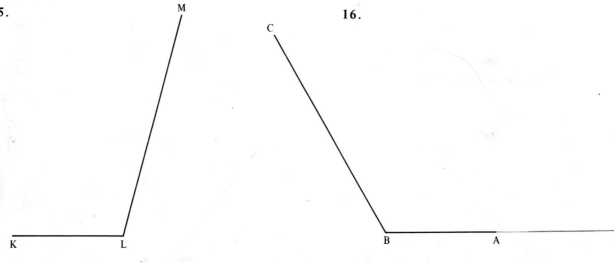

16.

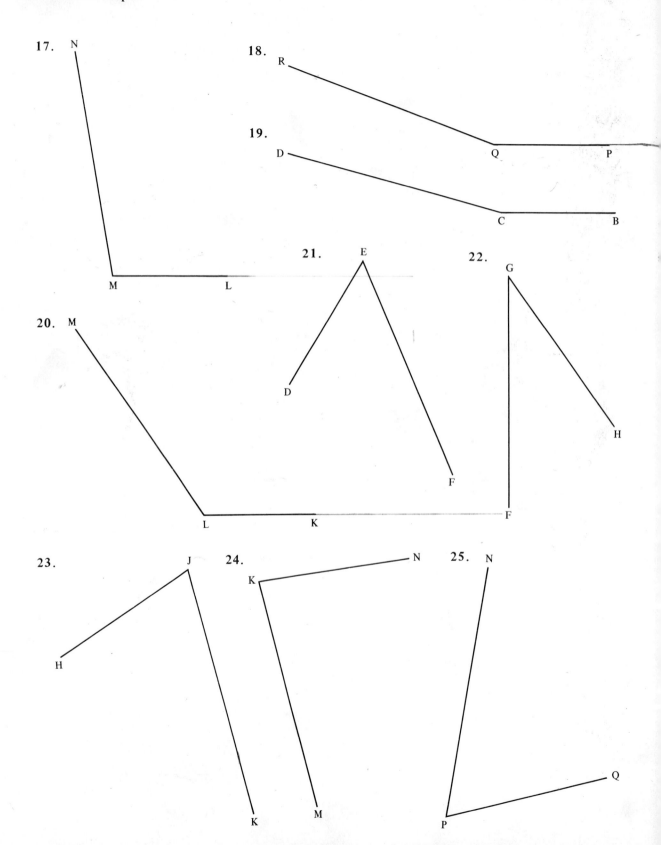

26. Measure the
angle *a* that
the kite string
makes with
the ground.

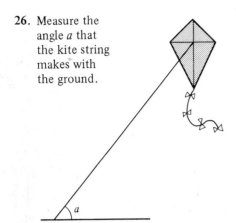

27. Measure the
angle *a* that
the ladder
makes with
the ground,
and the angle
b that the
ladder makes
with the wall.

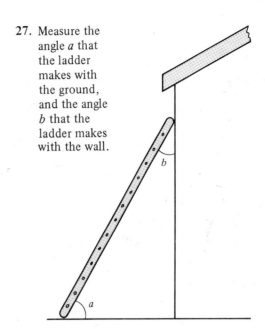

28. Measure the
angle *a* that
the diagonal
board makes
with the
horizontal and
the angle *b*
that the diagonal
board makes
with the vertical.

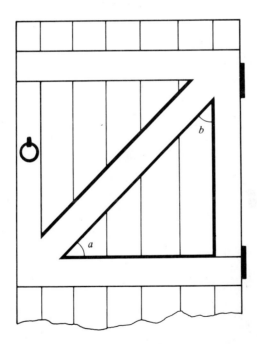

Example 3

Using a protractor, draw a) $A\hat{B}C = 50°$, b) $X\hat{Y}Z = 170°$.

a) 1. Draw the straight line **AB**. Make it 6 cm long.
    2. Place the protractor on the paper with its base line on the line **AB** and
        its centre point **W** on **B** as shown.
    3. Mark the point **C** at 50° on the scale starting from 0° at **A**.
    4. Join **BC**, and the angle 50° is now drawn complete.

a)

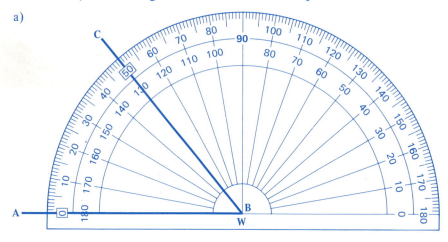

b) 1. Draw the straight line **XY**. Make
        it 6 cm long.
    2. Place the protractor on the paper with its
        base line on the line **XY** and its centre point **W** on **Y** as shown.
    3. Mark the point **Z** at 170° on the scale starting from 0° at **X**.
    4. Join **YZ** and the angle of 170° is now drawn complete.

b)

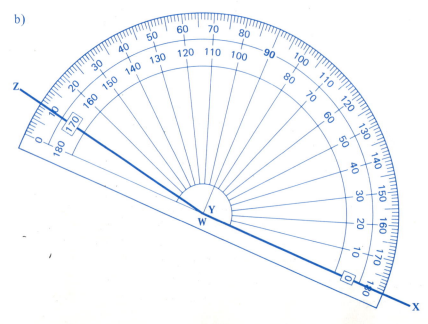

Exercise 86

For each question, draw a line AB 6 cm long. Then draw the angle.

1. Draw $A\hat{B}C$ equal to $60°$
2. Draw $A\hat{B}C$ equal to $40°$
3. Draw $A\hat{B}C$ equal to $45°$
4. Draw $A\hat{B}C$ equal to $65°$
5. Draw $A\hat{B}C$ equal to $35°$
6. Draw $B\hat{A}C$ equal to $30°$
7. Draw $B\hat{A}C$ equal to $80°$
8. Draw $B\hat{A}C$ equal to $50°$
9. Draw $B\hat{A}C$ equal to $55°$
10. Draw $B\hat{A}C$ equal to $25°$

11. Draw $A\hat{B}C$ equal to $120°$
12. Draw $A\hat{B}C$ equal to $150°$
13. Draw $A\hat{B}C$ equal to $155°$
14. Draw $A\hat{B}C$ equal to $125°$
15. Draw $A\hat{B}C$ equal to $115°$
16. Draw $B\hat{A}C$ equal to $130°$
17. Draw $B\hat{A}C$ equal to $110°$
18. Draw $B\hat{A}C$ equal to $140°$
19. Draw $B\hat{A}C$ equal to $145°$
20. Draw $B\hat{A}C$ equal to $95°$

For the following questions, draw a line PQ 7 cm long. Then draw the angle.

21. Draw $P\hat{Q}R$ equal to $48°$
22. Draw $P\hat{Q}R$ equal to $22°$
23. Draw $P\hat{Q}R$ equal to $63°$
24. Draw $P\hat{Q}R$ equal to $79°$
25. Draw $P\hat{Q}R$ equal to $8°$
26. Draw $Q\hat{P}R$ equal to $87°$
27. Draw $Q\hat{P}R$ equal to $136°$
28. Draw $Q\hat{P}R$ equal to $161°$
29. Draw $Q\hat{P}R$ equal to $114°$
30. Draw $Q\hat{P}R$ equal to $157°$

Draw these angles. Choose a suitable length for the lines.

31. $E\hat{F}G = 75°$
32. $G\hat{H}J = 82°$
33. $J\hat{K}L = 96°$
34. $L\hat{M}N = 12°$
35. $M\hat{N}P = 143°$
36. $P\hat{Q}R = 178°$

Example 4

Draw a triangle with AB = 5 cm, $\hat{A} = 50°$ and $\hat{B} = 70°$. Measure the third angle.

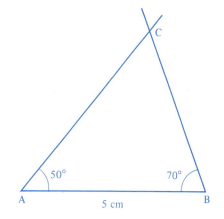

By measurement, $\hat{C} = 60°$

Exercise 87

For each question, draw the triangle ABC from the details given. Then measure the angle $\hat{C}$ with a protractor.

1. AB = 5 cm, $\hat{A} = 40°$, $\hat{B} = 60°$
2. AB = 5 cm, $\hat{A} = 30°$, $\hat{B} = 80°$
3. AB = 5 cm, $\hat{A} = 50°$, $\hat{B} = 40°$
4. AB = 5 cm, $\hat{A} = 60°$, $\hat{B} = 90°$
5. AB = 5 cm, $\hat{A} = 50°$, $\hat{B} = 50°$
6. AB = 5 cm, $\hat{A} = 60°$, $\hat{B} = 60°$
7. AB = 6 cm, $\hat{A} = 30°$, $\hat{B} = 40°$
8. AB = 6 cm, $\hat{A} = 40°$, $\hat{B} = 40°$
9. AB = 6 cm, $\hat{A} = 50°$, $\hat{B} = 100°$
10. AB = 6 cm, $\hat{A} = 20°$, $\hat{B} = 110°$

For each question, draw the triangle. Then measure the size of the third angle with a protractor.

11. PQ = 7 cm, $Q\hat{P}R = 38°$, $P\hat{Q}R = 71°$
12. AB = 6 cm, $A\hat{B}C = 115°$, $B\hat{A}C = 22°$
13. EF = 5 cm, $E\hat{F}G = 77°$, $F\hat{E}G = 42°$
14. UV = 6 cm, $T\hat{U}V = 124°$, $U\hat{V}T = 12°$
15. XY = 8 cm, $X\hat{Y}Z = 32°$, $Y\hat{X}Z = 68°$

5.3   Line symmetry

If you can fold a shape down the middle so that one half fits exactly over the other, then the shape is said to be *symmetrical*. The fold line is called its *axis or line of symmetry*.

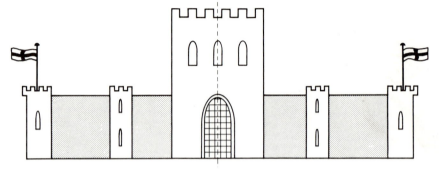

Example 1

Which one of the following shapes is different from the others, that is to say, not symmetrical?

a)   b)   c)

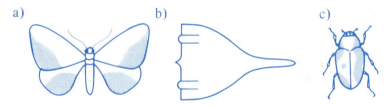

The one that is different is c) because the left-hand side is not exactly the same as the right-hand side.

Exercise 88

For each of the following find which shape is different from the others, i.e. not symmetrical.

1.   a)   b)   c)

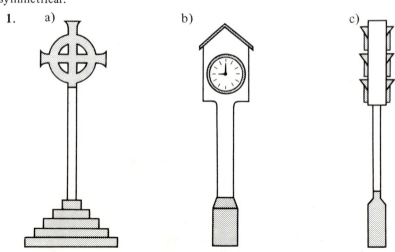

2. a)

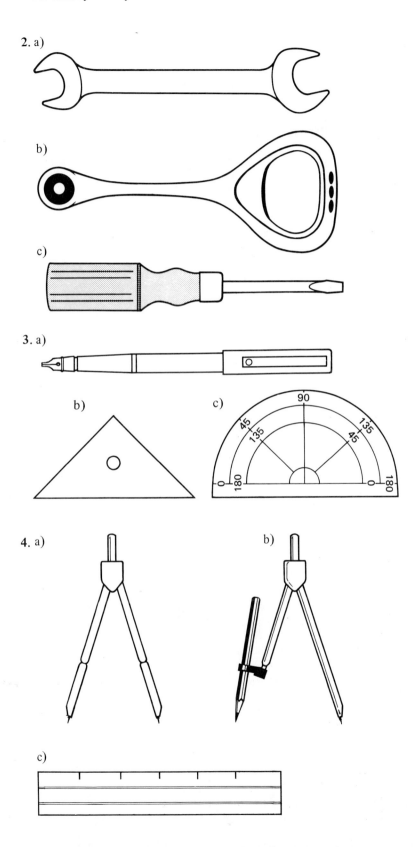

b)

c)

3. a)

b)

c)

4. a)   b)

c)

5. a) 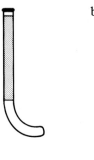　b) 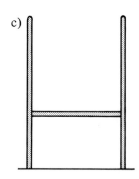　c)

6. a)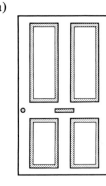

b)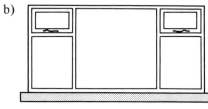

c)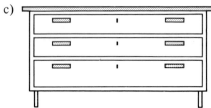

7. a) 　b) 　c)

Some shapes have more than one axis or line of symmetry. For example a three-leaf clover has three lines of symmetry.

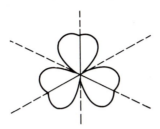

Example 2

Which one of the following shapes has only one line of symmetry.

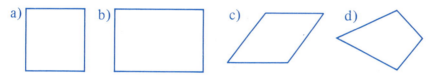

The answer is d) because the other shapes have more than one line of symmetry. Look at the diagrams below.

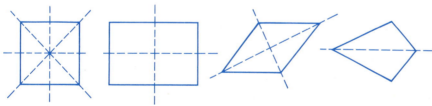

Exercise 89

For each question, find which shape has only one line of symmetry.

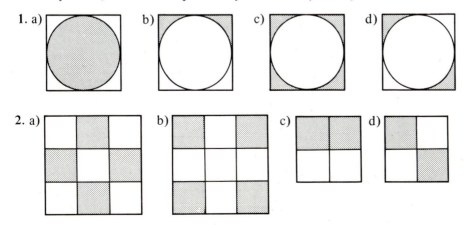

3. a)

b)

c)

d)

4. a)

b)

c)

d)

5. a)

b)

c)

d)

6. a)

b)

c)

d)

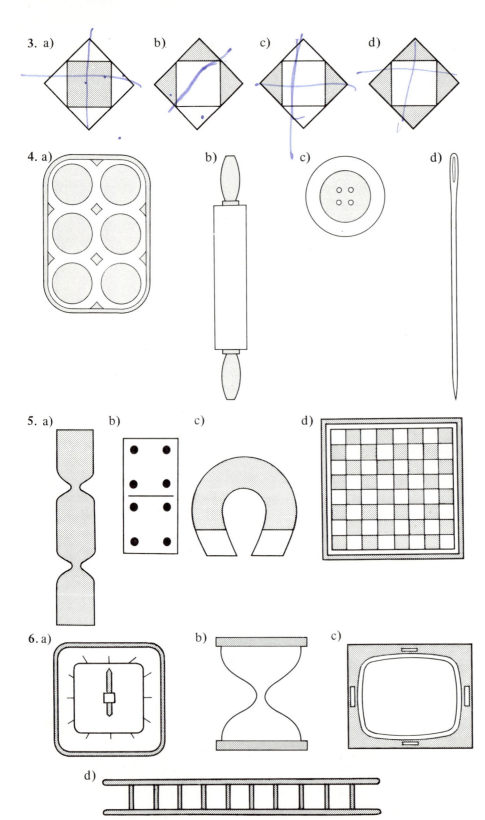

5.4   Solid shapes _____

Many well known objects are solids with mathematical names:

A sugar lump is a *cube*

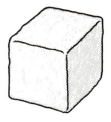

A match box is a
cuboid

A tin of beans is
a *cylinder*

Some tents are *triangular prisms*

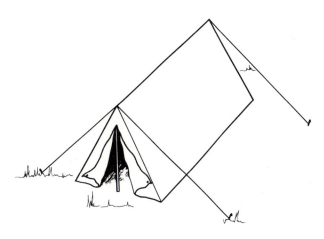

A dunce's cap is
a *cone*

A football is a *sphere*

Exercise 90

For each of the following, copy and complete the sentences by inserting the appropriate mathematical name.

1. A dice is a . . . .

2. A brick is a . . . .

3. A stick of seaside rock is a tall, thin . . . .

4. A beefburger is a . . . . which is nearly flat.

5. A cricket ball is a . . . .

6. A record is a . . . .

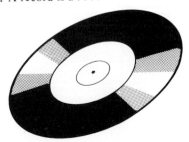

7. The piece of wood which is holding the door open is a . . . .

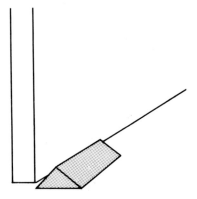

8. The ice cream is
in a . . . .

9. When this wine glass is
filled, the wine is
poured into a . . . .

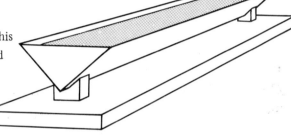

10. When water is poured into this
drinking trough, it is poured
into a . . . .

11. A cricket stump is a long,
thin . . . . with a . . . . at
one end.

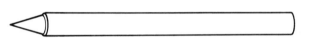

What mathematical name best describes each of these
solid objects?

12. A packet of washing powder.
13. The Moon.
14. The roof section of a house.

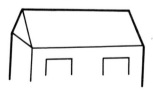

15. A drain-pipe.
16. The nose of a rocket.
17. A paperback book.
18. A ball bearing.

19. A chimney. (Give two names.)

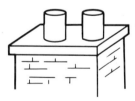

20. A hot water tank. (Give two names.)

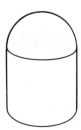

Investigation 5

Paper Folding

1. Take a piece of paper. Fold it in half. Draw a shape next to the fold line.

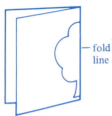

Cut round your shape. Unfold the paper. You should now have a symmetrical shape with *one* axis of symmetry.

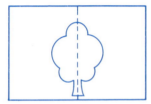

2. Repeat question 1. Draw a different shape this time. Is your cut-out symmetrical? How many axes of symmetry does it have?

3. By folding your paper in half and drawing the right lines, can you cut out shapes like the capital letters of the alphabet? Are there any letters that cannot be made in this way?

4. Take a piece of paper and fold it in half. Now fold it in half again. (Look at the diagram below.) Draw a shape along the folded edges. Cut it out and open it up. How many axes of symmetry does your cut-out have?

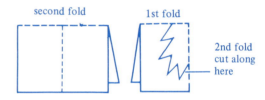

5. Fold a piece of paper in half, and again, as in question 4. Now fold it a third time as shown in the diagram below. Draw and cut out a shape. How many axes of symmetry does it have?

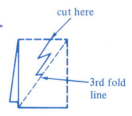

6. Can you fold your paper in such a way that it will give your cut-out *three on six* axes of symmetry? Investigate this problem and explain your answer?

6 Graphs

6.1 Ordered pairs

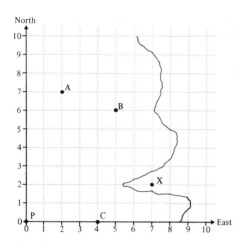

If you are standing at point P shown on the map, the position of any other place on the map can be fixed by giving the following two distances.

a) the distance East of P

b) the distance North of P

On the above map, A is the point 2 km East of P and 7 km North of P. The position is usually given by the *ordered pair* (2, 7). In the same way the ordered pair for the point B is (5, 6); the ordered pair for the point C is (4, 0).

The order of the numbers is important because (7, 2) would give the point X and not the point A.

Exercise 91

1. Look at the places that are marked on the map, then copy and complete the details below.

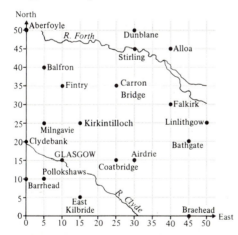

Barrhead (0, 10)   Coatbridge (25, 15)
Clydebank (   )   Carron Bridge (   )
Aberfoyle (   )   Airdrie (   )
Pollokshaws (5, 10)   Stirling (   )
Milngavie (   )   Dunblane (   )
Balfron (   )   Falkirk (   )
Glasgow (10, 15)   Alloa (   )
Fintry (   )   Braehead (   )
East Kilbride (   ) Bathgate (   )
Kirkintilloch (,) Linlithgow (   )

2. Look at the places that are marked on the map, then copy and complete the details below.

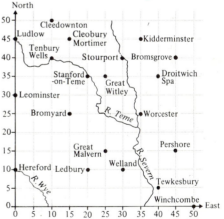

Hereford (0, 10)   Great Witley (   )
Leominster (   )   Welland (   )
Ludlow (   )   Stourport (   )
Tenbury Wells (10, 40)   Worcester (   )
Cleedownton (   )   Kidderminster (   )
Bromyard (   )   Tewkesbury (   )
Cleobury Mortimer (   ) Droitwich Spa (   )
Ledbury (   )   Pershore (   )
Stanford-on-Teme (   ) Bromsgrove (   )
Great Malvern (   )   Winchcombe (   )

3. Look at the theatre seats which have been reserved. Copy and complete the details below by giving the ordered pair for each child's seat.

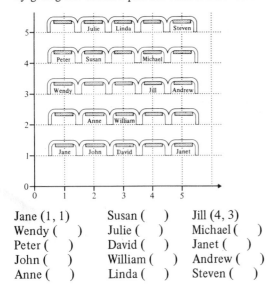

Jane (1, 1)   Susan (   )   Jill (4, 3)
Wendy (   )   Julie (   )   Michael (   )
Peter (   )   David (   )   Janet (   )
John (   )   William (   )   Andrew (   )
Anne (   )   Linda (   )   Steven (   )

4. Copy the map below and mark all the places whose ordered pairs are given in the table.

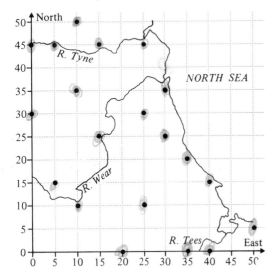

Consett (0, 30)
Sedgefield (25, 10)
Prudhoe (0, 45)
Houghton-le-Spring (25, 30)
Crook (5, 15)
Jarrow (25, 45)
Ryton (5, 45)
Easington Village (30, 25)
Bishop Auckland (10, 10)

Sunderland (30, 35)
Stanley (10, 35)
Stockton-on-Tees (35, 0)
Newcastle Airport (10, 50)
Blackhall Colliery (35, 20)
Durham (15, 25)
Middlesbrough (40, 0)
Newcastle (15, 45)
Hartlepool (40, 15)
Coatham Mundeville (20, 0)
Redcar (50, 5)

5. A leisure company applies for permission to build holiday chalets on the coast. Unfortunately the company executive forgot where. He knew it was either (40, 30) or (40, 40) or (30, 40) or (30, 30). Look at the map in question 4 and decide which is correct.

The position of a point on a graph is fixed by referring to its ordered pair. The distances for each point along the axes are measured from a fixed point 0, called the origin.
The horizontal line from 0 is called the x-axis.
The vertical line from 0 is called the y-axis.

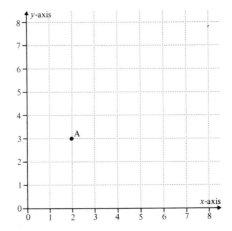

The position of any point given by the ordered pair (x, y) is the point which is x units to the 'east' of the origin and y units to the 'north' of the origin.
On the graph shown above, the ordered pair (2, 3) gives the position of the point A.

Example 1

Give the ordered pairs necessary to fix the position of each point shown in the diagram.

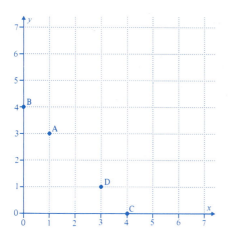

A is the point $(1, 3)$
B is the point $(0, 4)$
C is the point $(4, 0)$
D is the point $(3, 1)$

Example 2

On graph paper, with the x-axis numbered from 0 to 10 and the y-axis numbered from 0 to 8, plot the positions of the following points.

$(1, 4), (1, 6), (3, 8), (5, 6), (5, 4), (7, 4), (7, 6),$
$(9, 7), (10, 6), (9, 6), (9, 4), (8, 3), (8, 0),$
$(7, 2), (5, 0), (5, 1), (3, 3), (3, 2), (1, 4)$

Join each point to the next with a straight line. Then suggest a name for the picture you have drawn.

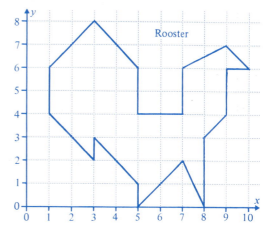

Exercise 92

Give the ordered pairs necessary to fix the position of each point shown in the diagram below.

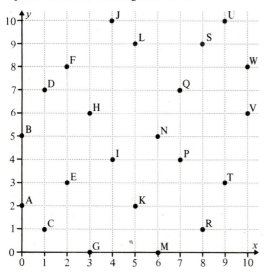

Exercise 93

On graph paper, with the x-axis numbered from 0 to 10 and the y-axis numbered from 0 to 8, plot the positions of the points in each question. Join each point to the next with a straight line. Then suggest a name for the picture you have drawn.

1. $(1, 2), (0, 4), (2, 4), (2, 5), (3, 5), (3, 6), (4, 6),$
   $(4, 5), (5, 5), (5, 6), (6, 6), (6, 5), (7, 5), (7, 4),$
   $(10, 4), (8, 2), (1, 2).$

2. $(5, 1), (5, 3), (0, 5), (0, 6), (5, 4), (5, 5), (10, 5),$
   $(10, 1), (5, 1).$

3. $(2, 0), (3, 1), (4, 1), (4, 4), (2, 4), (3, 8), (6, 8),$
   $(7, 4), (5, 4), (5, 1), (6, 1), (7, 0), (2, 0).$

4. $(2, 1), (3, 2), (4, 2), (4, 5), (0, 5), (0, 6), (4, 7),$
   $(4, 8), (5, 8), (5, 7), (9, 6), (9, 5), (5, 5), (5, 2),$
   $(6, 2), (7, 1), (5, 1), (5, 0), (4, 0), (4, 1), (2, 1).$

5. $(1, 4), (0, 4), (0, 7), (1, 7), (1, 6), (7, 6), (7, 7),$
   $(10, 7), (10, 4), (7, 4), (7, 5), (1, 5), (1, 4).$

6. $(1, 2), (1, 4), (0, 4), (0, 5), (7, 5), (8, 7), (9, 7),$
   $(10, 5), (10, 4), (9, 2), (8, 2), (7, 4), (3, 4), (3,2),$
   $(1, 2).$

7. $(2, 3), (1, 3), (0, 4), (1, 4), (1, 5), (0, 5), (1, 6),$
   $(2, 6), (3, 5), (7, 5), (8, 6), (9, 6), (10, 5), (8, 5),$
   $(8, 4), (10, 4), (9, 3), (8, 3), (7, 4), (3, 4), (2, 3).$

8. $(5, 8), (8, 6), (10, 6), (10, 5), (8, 5), (5, 3),$
   $(10, 3), (10, 2), (5, 2), (8, 0), (6, 0), (3, 2), (1, 2),$
   $(1, 3), (3, 3), (6, 5), (1, 5), (1, 6), (6, 6), (3, 8),$
   $(5, 8).$

For these two questions, use an x-axis numbered from 0 to 18 and a y-axis numbered from 0 to 18.

9. $(11, 9), (11, 10), (10, 11), (8, 11), (7, 10), (7, 8),$
   $(8, 7), (9, 7), (9, 5), (10, 5), (14, 4), (17, 3),$
   $(18, 2), (18, 1), (17, 2), (14, 3), (10, 4), (8, 4),$
   $(4, 3), (1, 2), (0, 1), (0, 2), (1, 3), (4, 4), (8, 5), (9, 5).$

10. $(4, 18), (4, 17), (5, 17), (5, 16), (6, 16), (5, 15),$
    $(5, 14), (6, 14), (5, 13), (5, 12), (6, 12), (5, 11),$
    $(4, 11), (4, 3), (5, 2), (5, 0), (2, 0), (2, 2), (3, 3),$
    $(3, 11), (2, 11), (1, 12), (2, 12), (2, 13), (1, 14),$
    $(2, 14), (2, 15), (1, 16), (2, 16), (2, 17), (3, 17),$
    $(3, 18), (4, 18).$

6.2 Plotting points

The axes of a graph may be drawn on both sides of the origin. The paper is then divided into four parts called quadrants.

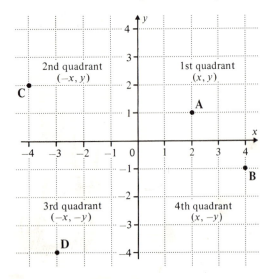

Distances to the right of the origin are positive.
Distances to the left of the origin are negative.
Distances upwards from the origin are positive.
Distances downwards from the origin are negative.

So both positive and negative values of x and y may be plotted; the ordered pair (x, y) which gives the position of any point is called its Cartesian coordinate.

Example 1

Write down the coordinates of the points A, B, C, and D, shown on the graph above.

A is the point $(2, 1)$
B is the point $(4, -1)$
C is the point $(-4, 2)$
D is the point $(-2, -4)$

Exercise 94

Write down the coordinates of the points shown on the following graph.

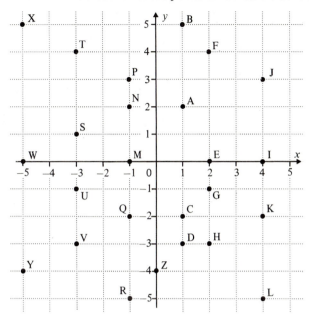

Example 2

Plot the following points and join each point to the next with a straight line. Suggest a name for the picture you have drawn.

$(2, -1), (2, -5), (3, -4),$
$(5, -4), (4, -5), (-3, -5),$
$(-1, -4), (-1, -2), (-3, 0),$
$(-2, 1), (-4, 3), (-4, 6),$
$(-2, 5), (0, 6), (0, 3),$
$(-1, 2), (2, -1).$

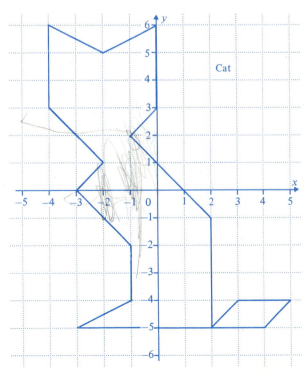

Cat

Exercise 95

On graph paper with the x-axis numbered from -5 to 5 and the y-axis numbered from -10 to 10, plot the positions of the points in each question. Join each point to the next with a straight line. Then suggest a name for the picture you have drawn.

1. $(1, 10), (1, 5), (2, 4), (2, -5), (1, -6), (0, -6), (-1, -5), (-1, 4), (0, 5), (0, 10),$
   $(1, 10).$

2. $(0, 10), (4, -1), (1, -1), (1, -2), (2, -2), (1, -6), (-1, -6), (-2, -2), (-1, -2),$
   $(-1, -1), (-4, -1), (0, 10).$

3. $(3, 10), (4, 9), (4, 7), (3, 6), (5, 6), (5, -6), (3, -6), (4, -7), (4, -9), (3, -10),$
   $(2, -9), (2, -7), (3, -6), (1, -6), (1, 6), (3, 6), (2, 7), (2, 9), (3, 10).$

4. $(0, 9), (3, 4), (1, 4), (1, -4), (3, -6) (3, -7), (1, -5), (1, -6), (3, -8), (3, -9),$
   $(1, -7), (1, -9), (-1, -9), (-1, -7), (-3, -9), (-3, -8), (-1, -6), (-1, -5),$
   $(-3, -7), (-3, -6), (-1, -4), (-1, 4), (-3, 4), (0, 9).$

5. $(1, 10), (1, -1), (2, 9), (3, 10), (4, 9), (4, -7), (3, -10), (3, -5), (4, -5), (3, -5),$
   $(3, 9), (2, -1), (2, -3), (-1, -3), (1, -3), (1, -7), (-1, -7), (1, -7), (0, -10),$
   $(-1, -7), (-1, -3), (-2, -3), (-2, -1), (1, -1), (-1, -1), (-1, 10), (1, 10).$

For questions **6** to **11**, draw a grid with both the x-axis and the y-axis numbered from -12 to 12.

6. $(4, 5), (4, 3), (5, 4), (6, 3), (6, 1), (5, 0), (4, 1), (4, -2), (3, -3), (7, -2), (7, -3),$
   $(3, -4), (-3, -4), (-7, -3), (-7, -2), (-3, -3), (3, -3), (-3, -3), (-4, -2),$
   $(-4, 5), (4, 5).$

7. $(2, 4), (3, 5), (7, 5), (8, 1), (9, 1), (10, -1), (9, -3), (7, -5), (-1, -5), (-6, -4),$
   $(-7, 0), (-4, 1), (8, 1), (3, 1), (2, 2), (2, 3), (-10, 4) (2, 4).$

8. $(2, 5), (4, 5), (6, 4), (7, 1), (7, -4), (6, -5), (5, -5), (6, -4), (6, 0), (5, -1),$
   $(4, 0), (2, 2), (4, 4), (5, 2), (5, 3), (6, 3), (6, 2), (5, 2), (5, 1), (4, 0), (4, -5),$
   $(5, -6), (2, -6) (2, -1), (-5, -1), (-6, -2), (-6, -5), (-5, -6), (-7, -6),$
   $(-8, -1), (-8, 1), (-7, 3), (-3, 4), (0, 4), (2, 5).$

9. $(8, 4), (9, 3), (10, 3), (11, 2), (11, -4), (10, -6), (9, -6), (10, -4), (10, 2), (9, 2),$
   $(9, 0), (8, -1), (9, -4), (8, -9), (7, -9), (8, -4), (6, -2), (7, -4), (6, -9), (5, -9),$
   $(6, -4), (5, -2), (-1, -2), (-1, -8), (-2, -9), (-3, -9), (-2, -8), (-2, -3),$
   $(-3, 0), (-3, -8), (-4, -9), (-5, -9), (-4, -8), (-4, 0), (-7, 5), (-8, 5),$
   $(-10, 3), (-11, 3), (-12, 4), (-12, 5), (-10, 7), (-10, 6), (-9, 6), (-10, 7),$
   $(-9, 8), (-9, 9), (-8, 8), (-7, 8), (-1, 4), (8, 4).$

10. $(2, 4), (0, 6), (4, 10), (6, 8), (0, 2), (2, 0), (2, 4), (2, 0), (4, 2), (8, -2), (6, -4),$
    $(2, 0), (2, -4), (3, -10), (-3, -10), (-2, -4), (0, -2), (-2, 0), (0, -2), (-4, -6),$
    $(-6, -4), (0, 2), (-2, 4), (-2, 0), (-2, 4), (-4, 2), (-8, 6), (-6, 8), (-2, 4),$
    $(-2, 6), (-1, 7), (1, 7).$

11. $(-9, -12), (-9, 11), (-10, 12), (-6, 12), (-7, 11), (-7, 10), (-6, 9), (-6, -3),$
    $(-6, 9), (2, 9), (2, 4), (-6, 4), (2, 4), (2, 9), (4, 9), (4, 4), (12, 4), (4, 4), (4, 9),$
    $(12, 9), (12, -3), (4, -3), (4, 2), (12, 2), (4, 2), (4, -3), (2, -3), (2, 2), (-6, 2),$
    $(2, 2), (2, -3), (-6, -3), (-7, -4), (-7, 10), (-7, -12).$

12. Draw some shapes of your own on graph paper with axes. List the coordinates of corners of the shapes.

Investigation 6A

Mazes

Find the way through this 5 by 5 maze. Write down the coordinates of each corner you go round.

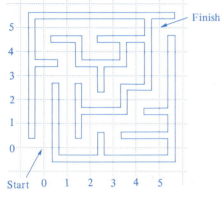

The path through the maze is

$(0, 0) \rightarrow (0, 3) \rightarrow (1, 3) \rightarrow (1, 0)$
$\rightarrow (2, 0) \rightarrow (2, 1) \rightarrow (4, 1) \rightarrow (4, 2)$
$\rightarrow (5, 2) \rightarrow (5, 5)$

Check the route.

1. Find the route through the following 10 by 10 maze. Write down the coordinates of each corner you go round.

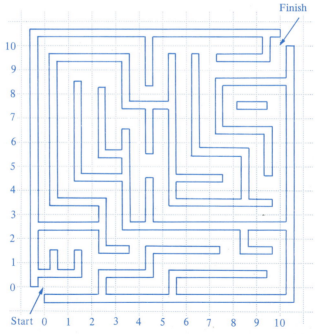

2. (a) Construct a 10 by 10 maze different from the above. On a separate sheet of paper write down the correct path. Get your neighbour to work out the correct path. Check that the answers agree.

   (b) Can you construct a 10 by 10 maze, which starts at $(0, 0)$ and finishes at $(10, 10)$ and whose path passes through every point?

   (c) Can you construct a 10 by 10 maze, which starts at $(0, 0)$ and finishes at $(10, 10)$ and whose path passes through every point?

Investigation 6B

1. Andrea, Brian, Claire, and David decide to have a race to the centre of the maze.
Each one starts at a different place.

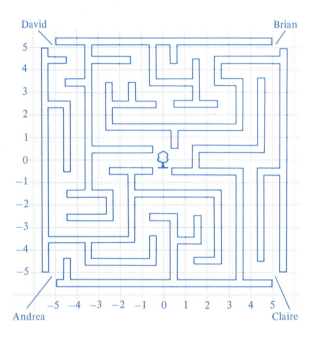

a) Find the route each will take and write down the coordinates of each corner
on the route.
b) The side of each square is 2 m.
Calculate the distance each person will have to travel to reach the centre of
the maze.

2. a) Can you construct a 10 by 10 maze with four entry points with the following
restrictions:
i) the four routes finish at the centre,
ii) the routes do not overlap,
iii)every point is on one or other of the routes.
b) Repeat a), but finish at a point different from the origin, with the
same restrictions:
i)   the four routes finish at the centre,
ii)   the routes do not overlap,
iii) every point is on one or other of the routes.

7 Relationships

7.1 Sentences

A sentence can be either true or false.

Example 1

'The sum of 6 and 4 is 11' is false.
'There are 7 days in a week' is true.

Exercise 96

State whether each sentence is true or false:

1. The sum of 7 and 8 is 15.
2. June has 31 days.
3. 16 is four less than 20.
4. The time 2.45 is the same as a quarter to three.
5. There are 100 mm in 1 m.
6. $\frac{6}{7} = \frac{3}{4}$
7. At least 5 coins are needed to make up 45p.
8. April is six months after October.
9. There are 8 prime numbers less than 20.
10. 100 kg = 1 tonne

An open sentence is a sentence which may be true *or* false. You need more information to decide which.

Example 2

a) $*$ is a month with 30 days.
   If we replace $*$ with November, the sentence now reads, 'November is a month with 30 days.' This is a true statement.

   November is a *replacement* for $*$ that has made the sentence true.

   December is a replacement for $*$ that would make the sentence false. This month has 31 days.

b) $\square + 7 = 10$
   Replace $\square$ with 5, i.e. make $\square = 5$
   This makes the sentence false, because 5 and 7 does not equal 10. But make $\square = 3$ and the sentence is true, because $3 + 7 = 10$.

Exercise 97

For each open sentence find a replacement which will make the sentence a true statement.

1. $\square + 2 = 7$
2. $12 - * = 3$
3. $\triangle$ is a month with 31 days.
4. $*$ is bigger than 10
5. $\triangle - 5 = 9$
6. $\square$ is 10 minutes after 2.55
7. $10 + \square = 21$
8. $\triangle$ is the day after Wednesday
9. $*$ is smaller than 20
10. $15 - \triangle = 9$
11. $\frac{*}{6} = \frac{1}{2}$
12. $3000 \text{ kg} = \square$ tonnes
13. $8 + \triangle = 8$
14. $*$ is a month with less than 31 days
15. $\square$ cm is twice as long as 9 cm
16. $400 \text{ cm} = \square$ metres
17. $\square + \square = 10$
18. $\triangle + * = 4$

Open sentences in words often need to be changed to a shorter form.

Example 3

Write this sentence in shorter form.
When a number is added to 5 the answer is 9.

In shorter form the sentence becomes
$$5 + \square = 9$$

Exercise 98

Write these open sentences in shorter form.

1. When 3 is added to a number the answer is 8.
2. When a number is subtracted from 10 the result is 4.
3. When 8 is subtracted from a number the result is 11.
4. When a number is added to 9 the answer is 26.
5. The number of mm in 3 m is x.
6. When a number is added to itself the result is 24.
7. The sum of two different numbers is 20.
8. The difference of two numbers is 6.

7.2 Equations

An open sentence with an '=' sign is called an equation.

In equations, a small letter usually stands for the unknown part of the open sentence.

Finding the replacement which makes the open sentence a true statement is called solving the equation.

Example 1

Solve these equations.

a) $x + 5 = 7$ b) $x - 4 = 3$
c) $10 - x = 3$

a) $x + 5 = 7$
    $x = 2$ because $2 + 5 = 7$
b) $x - 4 = 3$
    $x = 7$ because $7 - 4 = 3$
c) $10 - x = 3$
    $x = 7$ because $10 - 7 = 3$

Exercise 99

Solve these equations.

1. $x + 2 = 5$ 2. $x + 4 = 6$ 3. $x + 6 = 9$
4. $x + 3 = 7$ 5. $x + 7 = 9$ 6. $6 + x = 8$
7. $2 + x = 6$ 8. $4 + x = 7$ 9. $3 + x = 6$
10. $2 + x = 9$ 11. $8 - x = 6$ 12. $6 - x = 2$
13. $7 - x = 5$ 14. $5 - x = 2$ 15. $8 - x = 3$
16. $9 - x = 6$ 17. $x - 2 = 3$ 18. $x - 3 = 5$
19. $x - 4 = 2$ 20. $x - 4 = 5$

Example 2

Solve these equations.

a) $p - 4 = 10$ b) $8 - m = 3$
c) $y + y = 16$

a) $p - 4 = 10$
    $p = 14$ because $14 - 4 = 10$
b) $8 - m = 3$
    $m = 5$ because $8 - 5 = 3$
c) $y + y = 16$
    $y = 8$ because $8 + 8 = 16$

Exercise 100

Solve these equations.

1. $x + 3 = 5$ 2. $x + 5 = 9$ 3. $x + 2 = 8$
4. $y + 3 = 9$ 5. $y + 4 = 8$ 6. $z + 2 = 4$
7. $a + 1 = 9$ 8. $b + 4 = 5$ 9. $c + 9 = 12$
10. $d + 4 = 10$ 11. $3 + x = 8$ 12. $5 + x = 7$

13. $4 + m = 9$ 14. $2 + n = 7$ 15. $1 + p = 8$
16. $8 + q = 9$ 17. $4 + r = 12$ 18. $7 + s = 10$
19. $9 + t = 11$ 20. $10 + u = 12$ 21. $19 + x = 22$
22. $x - 7 = 10$ 23. $y - 9 = 4$ 24. $z - 6 = 17$

25. $14 - a = 9$ 26. $25 - b = 17$ 27. $16 - c = 4$
28. $l + l = 16$ 29. $x + x = 10$ 30. $z + z = 24$
31. $p + p = 7$ 32. $q + q = 21$ 33. $8 - y = y$
34. $24 - d = d$ 35. $n = 3 - n$ 36. $a + a = 36 - a$

Example 3

Look at the following sentence.
Form an equation and solve it.

When x is subtracted from 21 the result is 9.

The equation is

$$21 - x = 9$$
$$x = 12$$

Exercise 101

Form an equation and solve it for each of the following sentences.

1. When x is added to 4 the total is 9.
2. When 9 is added to y the result is 20.
3. When 7 is subtracted from z the answer is 4.
4. 5 less than b is 9.
5. c more than eight is thirteen.
6. When d is subtracted from 27 the result is 5.
7. When t is added to t the total is 36.
8. When a is added to one more than a the total is 13.
9. When f is added to f the total is 82.
10. When k is added to 12 the total is $k + k + k$.

Investigation 7

Clockwork counting

The clock has only one hour hand.
It is pointing at 3. Four hours later it will be
pointing at 7.

$$3 + 4 = 7$$

Also 4 hours after 10 o'clock it will be pointing
pointing at 2 o'clock.

$$10 + 4 = 2$$

The first answer fits in with normal counting,
but the second answer does not.

1. Find some more sums that do *not* work like
    normal counting.

2. Using the clock, copy and complete this table.

Hours added on

+	1	2	3	4	5	6
1				5		
2				6		
3				7		
4				8		
5				9		
6				10		
7				11		
8				12		
9	10	11	12	1	2	3
10				2		
11				3		
12				4		

(Starting time — left column label)

Using the clock, solve these equations.
Your answer will always be a number between
1 and 12.

3. $x + 2 = 7$ 4. $x + 3 = 8$
5. $x + 4 = 2$ 6. $x + 2 = 1$
7. $x + 7 = 3$ 8. $x + 5 = 4$
9. $x + 10 = 12$ 10. $x + 12 = 3$
11. $x + 8 = 2$ 12. $x + 6 = 1$
13. $x - 5 = 10$ 14. $x - 6 = 11$
15. $x - 3 = 12$ 16. $2 - x = 11$
17. $7 - x = 10$ 18. $1 - x = 9$
19. $10 - x = 6$ 20. $6 - x = 7$

In these equations there are two or more answers in
each case.
21. $x + x = 6$ 22. $x + x = 2$
23. $x + x = 10$ 24. $x + x + x = 3$

25. Find more situations where clockwork counting
     will apply.

e.g. a control switch

For each situation set up a table, as in question 2 and
make-up your own equation, as in questions 3 to 24.

Secondary Mathematics: Problems and Practice
Table of Contents